How to Stop Bullying in Your School

How to Stop Bullying in Your School

in

Your School

A guide for teachers

GEORGE VARNAVA

David Fulton Publishers

London

David Fulton Publishers Ltd
The Chiswick Centre, 414 Chiswick High Road, London W4 5TF

www.fultonpublishers.co.uk

First published in Great Britain by David Fulton Publishers 2002

Note: The right of George Varnava to be identified as the author of this work
has been asserted by him in accordance with the Copyright, Designs and
Patents Act 1988.

British Library Cataloguing in Publication Data
A catalogue record for this book is available from the British Library

ISBN 1–85346–938–6

Typeset by FiSH Books, London
Printed and bound in Great Britain by Bell & Bain Ltd, Glasgow

Contents

Acknowledgements

The preparation and publication of this book have benefited from the involvement of many teachers, support staff and school students, to all of whom I am most grateful. Together, the members of Ashburton High School gave me the most rewarding professional experience of my career and Elva Boutflower, Head teacher of Hope Valley School in Liverpool – the first 'Checkpoints' pilot school – was instrumental from the outset with creative involvement and encouraging feedback. Philip Marples, Head teacher of Sonning Common Primary School in Oxfordshire, gave valuable help by developing in practice the original ideas on intervention. James Wetz, Principal of Cotham School, Bristol and Derek Greenup, Head teacher of Park House School and Sports College made important contributions to case study material. Heather Hodgkinson, Maths Coordinator at Moatbridge School, Eltham, London, gave unfailing support and enthusiasm.

Thanks to the Forum on Children and Violence, its coordinator Will McMahon and the Gulbenkian Foundation (the original funding body for the Checkpoints project) a network has been formed that has led to professional collaboration within education and beyond in the development of supportive intervention. Dr Julie Shaughnessy, Senior Lecturer at the Roehampton University of Surrey has – through her work with trainee teachers – ensured that the book is securely founded in relevant research, remaining relevant to classrooms today. Daniel Vidal, Principal of the Collège Pablo Néruda in Bègles, France and Evaluator of the European Commission's 'CONNECT' investigation into violence in schools, has placed the work in the wider international context.

The help I have been able to call on at will has been invaluable. My wife Zoë, Senior Lecturer at the Roehampton University of Surrey, has always been ready to advise with her expertise in the fields of teacher training and the English language. My daughter Alice, doctorate student at the University of Cardiff, has remained on call for technical assistance and the guidance and encouragement from Jude Bowen, Senior Commissioning Editor for David Fulton Publishers has, throughout, ensured that the progress from plan to publication has been an enjoyable experience.

Foreword

Countering violence in schools is a complex problem for educational practitioners for a number of reasons: first in its identification, second in knowing how to manage different forms of violence within school and community settings, third in taking the right kind of action that will proactively manage change within the organisation to counter violence.

Ongoing research reported in the European Commission's CONNECT project focused on the scale of the problem facing practitioners in understanding the impact of violence at a number of levels, from – for example – the high profile investigations into violence (Hungerford, Dunblane, the Cleveland inquiry and the North Wales inquiry into abuse in children's homes) to incidents of violence in the school context and in home and community settings. There is a large problem which needs to be addressed and schools need support to enable them to take positive action.

This is also a central issue for Initial Teacher Education in preparing trainee teachers to develop an ethos and philosophy which will promote non-violence through positive intervention. *How to Stop Bullying in Your School* provides teachers and trainees with a practical intervention programme to promote positive strategies and extend good practice.

Dr Julie Shaughnessy
Senior Lecturer, University of Surrey, Roehampton
Research Co-ordinator, Strategy Against Violence in Education (SAVE)/
Birmingham LEA Research Evaluation into 'Checkpoints'

To Zoë

Introduction

We don't need to sit here talking about it, chatting about it. We need to get action now! And if we don't, this is going to carry on and if it carries on this world is not going to be a nice place.

(Seven-year-old Louise speaking at Circle time about bullying)

Supporting schools in tackling bullying

How to Stop Bullying in Your School is about taking action. It is also about listening to children. It describes the use and further development of an intervention programme designed to reduce bullying and violence in its various forms. The core of the book is a presentation of *Towards a Non-violent Society – Checkpoints for Schools* (Varnava 2000) and its companion *Towards a Non-violent Society – Checkpoints for Young People* (Varnava 2002).

In many children's minds, bullying and violence are synonymous. The original *Checkpoints* publications have been developed, however, in a climate of national concern over the specific problem of bullying. The publications have been widely used in schools and included in the initial and in-service training of teachers and other school staff. They are the product of firsthand experience in a variety of schools, are informed by research from Britain and abroad and benefit from close collaboration between the voluntary and education sectors. The *Checkpoints* project was also selected as one of three British projects submitted to the European Commission's Education and Culture Initiative research programme (DG XX 11/10/99) 'CONNECT' on violence in schools. This programme has evaluated all schemes selected and assessed their potential for adaptation and use in different member states.

How to Stop Bullying in Your School is primarily intended as a practical support for schools seeking to create a non-bullying culture, a culture in which the welfare of all members is protected and where everyone feels secure. The term 'bullying' is applied to a wide variety of unwelcome physical and non-physical assaults. Unfriendly or threatening looks, insults, rumour-spreading, name-calling, teasing, sexual advances, aggressive gestures, tripping up, pushing and physical assault are all described, by some children, as bullying. When reported to adults, however, these offences are not all acknowledged as bullying by those responsible for dealing with them.

Bullying is cruel: it is neither confined to schools nor is it associated with children alone. Anyone, anywhere, can be a bully or a victim – child or adult, in school or workplace. There is no simple 'photo-fit' picture of either the bully or the victim but one common characteristic of victims is their actual or presumed difference in some way from their peers. Their appearance, manner or attitudes may attract unwanted attention; they feel intimidated and retreat to wherever they can feel safe or escape notice. Many bullies, on the other hand, are actually seeking attention and resort to aggressive behaviour in order to gain recognition and approval. Many schools have applied this 'rule of thumb' to anticipate bullying, demonstrating that successful prevention is far better than an uncertain cure. Bullying is only one manifestation of the aggression and violent behaviour that permeate British society – behaviour consistently stimulated by the competitiveness that now pervades the world of education, leisure, commerce and the workplace. The Health and Safety Executive (HSE) reports that violence in the workplace is increasing and considers violence to be 'any incident in which a person is abused, threatened or assaulted in circumstances relating to their work'. A school is also a workplace and teachers' unions have publicised the increasing number of assaults on their members by parents, relatives or other adults. Some of these assaults are the result of students seeking revenge, possibly because of wrongful or disputed accusations, demonstrating the tendency for violence, and the fear of it, to breed violence.

The most severe cases of bullying are covered by the national media, attracting public attention but it is the so-called 'low-level violence', its widespread acceptance, and the fear of bullying that go unreported, the psychological pain usually lasting far longer than the physical. The damage done to a victim's feelings are easily underestimated or ignored. Solving society's problems cannot be left to schools alone but schools are well placed to tackle bullying. The Economic and Social Research Council (ESRC), in *The Violence-resilient School: A comparative study of schools and their environments* (Hewitt 2001) found:

> It was very evident from our research that school practices do make a clear difference in the extent to which a school is resilient to its own situated potential for the occurrence of violence. Of particular significance are:
> – the quality of relationships within schools – between staff and between staff and students;
> – the quality and extent of communications within schools – including, especially, staff–student communications over violent incidents;
> – the range of policies and practices for dealing with violence and its potential emergence;
> – the engagement with and relationship to the neighbourhood of the school and its communities of interest.

Schools have the resources, the structures, the experience and a captive audience. Their effectiveness can be greatly enhanced by the active participation of parents, governors and others associated with the school. Formal and informal links between the separate groups can prevent the school from becoming isolated or unsupported or allow important messages from home or school to be exploited by manipulative children. The part that the voluntary sector can play is especially valuable and an important aim of this book is to encourage collaboration between children's organisations and schools. Major resources are channelled through these organisations which deliver an impressive array of services, activities and help-lines for young people in need or at risk. There is much to gain from schools and the voluntary sector sharing objectives, working closely together in the interests of the young people they both serve.

Ensuring that schools are safe for children and adults was of major concern to teachers and parents well before the highly publicised incidents of recent years. In the glare of national publicity and debate in 1980 the first school security guards were introduced to protect an inner-city secondary from intruders. Now, in 2002, public awareness has been raised, anti-bullying policies and home–school agreements introduced, exclusion has become the main sanction used by schools to counter disruption and, in some cases, personal alarms are carried by teachers. Nevertheless, the prevalence of bullying is still widespread. Many schools are no longer places open to the public, gates are electronically controlled and police officers are located in those schools causing most concern. Children have the right to be educated in a safe environment and every member of the school community is equally entitled to that right. Bullying is an infringement of that entitlement. In schools where the rejection of bullying is a prominent feature, self-esteem, good conditions for learning and sound personal relationships become part of the school's ethos. It is becoming increasingly apparent that for many children only the school provides security in an unsettled and often hostile world. Children are subjected to powerful, often damaging influences outside school, but a school unwilling to turn a blind eye to threats, aggression or violence can equip its students with the skills to avoid such dangers.

Stop bullying: six phases in the process of intervention

Each of the first six chapters of this book is a practical step towards the elimination of bullying. Together, they form a process which can be applied in total, in part or adapted to suit a school's particular circumstances. Case studies and reference to other experience illustrate the process and effectiveness of intervention.

Chapter 1, *'Bullying in the wider context of violence in society – culture, neglect and the role of the school'*, explains how aggression, threatening behaviour and recourse to violence have, for many, become a way of life. A culture of violence has evolved from a variety of causes and the level of tolerance has risen. Bullying is one of the most prevalent forms of this violence, yet it is often dismissed as 'part of growing up'. Schools have a central role in tackling all forms of violence.

Chapter 2, *'A presentation of "Towards a Non-violent Society – Checkpoints for Schools"'* (Varnava 2000). The Checkpoints represent seven aspects of school life.

These are identified as: Home/School/Community, Values, Organisation, Environment, Curriculum, Training and a seventh which invites the school to add examples of its own practice not included in the preceding six Checkpoints.

Chapter 3 *'The Checkpoints web: an institutional self-audit designed for the assessment of current practice and guidance towards further action'* describes how to carry out an audit using the web diagram. The exercise provides a starting point for the school to undertake self-assessment and gives clear indications of where action might be taken.

Chapter 4 *'Establishing base-line assessment criteria for measuring progress'* provides a range of criteria which have been found to be in use in a variety of schools. These include national comparators between schools, such as exclusion or attendance rates, and criteria which are tailor-made to suit a particular school.

Chapter 5, *'From school to community – how schools take the lead in tackling violence'*, explains how schools lead the community against bullying. Extending anti-bullying measures beyond the school is of central importance. *Checkpoints for Young People* (Varnava 2002) ensures the involvement of students and serves as a useful channel of communication into the home.

Chapter 6 discusses *'Training – the professional development of staff and the personal development of students'*. Training is an essential element of any whole-school campaign against bullying. This section draws on the *Checkpoints* agendas for training and suggests how training sessions might be conducted.

Eight stages in an anti-bullying strategy

How to Stop Bullying in Your School is an intervention programme, aimed at raising awareness and may be used initially as an institutional self-auditing tool. Since every school is unique, the scheme can also serve as a model, adaptable to local needs and priorities. The process consists of eight stages:

1. A whole-school action plan and timetable are formulated, with all sectors of the school community represented in their construction.
2. A commitment is agreed, e.g. 'we aim to be a bullying-free school', and is integrated with whole-school aims, policies and school development plan.
3. The commitment is publicised internally and externally, providing a basis for collaboration with parents and the local community.
4. A practical programme, such as *Checkpoints*, is introduced.
5. The self-auditing exercise (Chapter 3) highlights areas in which current practice helps to prevent bullying and others where risks are exposed.
6. Action is taken to address risk areas.
7. A whole-school review of the process is undertaken.
8. In the light of experience, the school formulates its own criteria for evaluating progress and reducing bullying.

The process can also be aligned or integrated with Personal, Social and Health Education (PSHE), Citizenship and the National Healthy School Standard and, ideally, be extended to permeate the whole school curriculum.

1 Bullying in the wider context of violence in society – culture, neglect and the role of the school

A culture of violence

Violence is commonly defined as 'behaviour which causes physical or psychological harm'. Violent attitudes and behaviour – in addition to reported crimes of violence and which are much more widespread – include bullying, domestic violence, child abuse, sexual assault and the newer categories of 'football hooliganism', 'road-rage', 'air-rage', 'trolley-rage' and now 'electronic bullying'. The most extreme acts of violence raise public concern but the prevalence of low-level, routine violence is rarely acknowledged or addressed. Such behaviour has become tolerated, unreported because it is not news. According to Secretary of State Jack Straw, we have become 'a walk-on-by society', believing that it is wiser not to interfere in someone else's business and that law and order are matters only for the police. The issue of violence involving children has recently been debated in the House of Lords. Lord Eames, Primate of Northern Ireland, introducing the debate to consider the current protection of children and young people in the United Kingdom said:

> Hardly a day passes without detailed media coverage of suffering children in some form: neglected or unprotected children; children from broken homes; children living or, should I say, existing in areas of poverty or social neglect; abused children, and especially children abused by those supposedly caring for them; and unwanted children, to say nothing of those young people who find themselves before our courts on serious charges...The children of the world are this generation's global face of tragedy...Today, almost one-third of our children, some 3.9 million, live in relative poverty.
>
> (*Hansard* 24 April 2002: Columns 309, 310)

Violence is endemic in British society and most of us fear it. It permeates our lives, our culture and our language. As a matter of routine, we use language that conveys aggression and we use violent words metaphorically to animate both speech and text. Workplace gossip becomes 'back-stabbing', political rivalry is reported as 'character assassination', business competition is 'cut-throat', to see Pavarotti many would 'kill for a ticket', we are flattered to have been 'head-hunted' and – most commonly – the written word is arranged with 'bullet points'. Nowhere more than in the confrontational exchanges in political circles is this use of inappropriate words and phrases more evident. Here is a compilation of authentic examples of violent vocabulary used by political commentators and politicians including the Prime Minister:

> Coming under fire, the Prime Minister returned to the offensive and squared up for a fight. Although his arguments were shot down in flames, he drew blood in the fight over taxes and punched home his attack on the Eurosceptics, declaring 'such pussyfooting will not staunch the blitzkrieg'. He declined a TV shoot-out and announced a further battery of weapons to crack down on youth crime, leaving the Chancellor to call up a grey army of volunteers.

There is ample evidence of violence in British and other societies. A large-scale study from the University of Bergen (Olweus 1993) found:

- a highly disturbing increase in the prevalence of violence and other anti-social behaviour in most industrialised societies;
- in some schools the risk of being bullied was up to four or five times greater than in other schools within the same community;
- no school can be regarded as bully-proof.

The study also found as relevant factors:

- child-rearing dimensions: negativism, permissiveness, power-assertive methods.

France and Germany, in particular, have recently expressed concerns over violence in schools and Germany has become the most recent addition to the growing number of countries legislating for a ban on all physical punishment. These include Austria, Croatia, Israel, Cyprus, Latvia, Denmark, Norway, Finland and Sweden. Sweden, which was the first country to introduce the ban in 1979, distributed a pamphlet to all homes bearing the following announcement:

> The law forbids all forms of physical punishment of children, including smacking, etc., although it goes without saying that you can still snatch a child away from a hot stove or open window if there is a risk of its injuring itself.

In the House of Lords debate on the protection of children and young people, Baroness Walmesley said:

> In December last year, the Government announced: 'We do not believe that any further change to the law at this time would command widespread public support or that it would be capable of consistent enforcement. However, we will keep the reasonable chastisement defence under review.' I wish to put the case for that review and to ask for a change of heart, based on the evidence. Why do we need a change in the law? We need it in order to give children the same protection under the law on assault as adults. It is as simple as that.
>
> (*Hansard* 24 April 2002: Column 332)

Whether British society is more or less violent than elsewhere and more or less violent than in the past is not the main issue; this is an unproductive line of enquiry. The crucial question is whether or not the level of violence is acceptable. A survey of childhood experience conducted by the National Society for the Prevention of Cruelty to Children (NSPCC) in England reveals that nearly all children have been smacked and one in five under-16s has been hit with an instrument. The national debate on parental smacking is gaining pace and will continue until the law on 'reasonable chastisement' is changed and children afforded the same protection under the law against all forms of physical assault as the protection enjoyed by adults. A six-year-old boy talking in a Radio 4 interview about how it felt to be smacked, said: 'a smack hurts. It makes you want to smack back.'

In the year 2000, a national poll found that 51 per cent of parents favoured a return to corporal punishment in schools. That is lower than in previous surveys but one might reasonably conclude that the majority want their children beaten and choose to leave it to teachers to carry out the punishment. Alternatively, one might interpret the finding as indicating that – for the sake of good order and the safety of their own children – parents only want other children beaten. The International Red Cross works at the extremes of 'man's inhumanity to man'. One of its main concerns is the cruel practice of using child soldiers, one of the most inhuman forms of exploitation. Television has brought startling images of guerrilla forces led by 12-year-olds in third-world countries yet Britain has also been condemned by a coalition of European states for sending boys of 17 into combat.

Education is by no means the only public service to be concerned with bullying. An article in the *Observer* newspaper (Summerskill 2002) reported on the widespread abuse of employees in the National Health Service (NHS) leading to nervous breakdowns and symptoms of post-traumatic stress.

Bullying in the workplace has long been a blight on the business world and an embarrassment to uniformed services, including the police and the Army. But new research confirms it has become just as prevalent in the 'caring' professions. Psychologist Noreen Tehrani, who carried out the survey, said 'it is disturbing to find such widespread abuse identified among people whose jobs are caring for others. In organisations where people are forced to do more and more, bullying appears to become more prevalent.' (Summerskill 2002).

This situation is mirrored across the education service where the teaching profession as a whole has itself felt bullied because of incessant waves of reform, bureaucratic pressures and the condemnatory treatment teachers have suffered.

The roots of violence lie in childhood; not because violence is natural but because it is learnt and it is largely learnt from adults. We condition children to believe that violence is an acceptable and effective means to an end. We give them an agenda for life that glamorises shopping, leisure and sex and they grow out of childhood with attitudes and behaviour that reflect that early learning. Research undertaken in Glasgow and North London found that nearly half the men surveyed thought that rape was acceptable in certain circumstances and a quarter of the men thought that it was justifiable to hit a woman (Zero Tolerance Trust 1999). It is not only those who have suffered physical punishment in childhood who later resort to violence; there are many factors at work: poverty, neglect, abuse, media influence and consumerism are among the most damaging. Children have been targeted as a vulnerable, profitable market. Even those too young to comprehend what is happening to them are not exempt: many of their toys, games and clothing are inspired by violence. Some countries, such as Norway, have acknowledged the potential and actual damage to children and now have legislation in place to prohibit advertising specifically aimed at children.

Violence and entertainment

Whether or not TV violence influences social behaviour continues to be a matter for debate. In 1998, The British Broadcasting Corporation, the Broadcasting Standards Commission and the Independent Television Commission published a joint report on violence in television. Its introduction stated: 'Violence is a fact of life. So long as it exists in society and the world, television programmes should reflect it and report it, both in fact and fiction. To do otherwise would be a substantial disservice to society.' The report makes much of the efforts of broadcasters to provide information for viewers on three matters: the role of the nine o'clock watershed, the use of advance warnings and the meaning of classification systems. It further 'recommends the launch of a national strategy, with an emphasis on the early acquisition of critical viewing skills among young viewers'. Nowhere does the report even contemplate the possibility of a reduction in the amount of violence shown. Since the publication of the report, it has been found that a fifth of all parents with children under ten routinely ignore the watershed and that more than a third of children have a television in their own bedroom. Film director Lord Puttnam is convinced of the media's potential for harmful influence:

> For too long, we have been prepared to accept, almost without question, a mainstream culture of film-making in which the consequences of actions, and in particular violent actions, are almost never addressed. The kinds of films we make shape people's view of the world; in this sense they are never value-free, most especially when they pretend to be. For the sake of the future health and prosperity of society, it behoves us to face up to this reality, and address it.

(*The Big Issue*, 460, October 2001, 22–8)

The distinctions drawn between the aims of the BBC's original mission statement 'to inform, to educate, to entertain' have become blurred. Makers of educational programmes hoping to motivate, try to make learning fun and – as a reaction to the predisposition of the media to focus on bad news stories – soap operas have begun to treat serious social issues within the framework of popular entertainment. School holidays are a time when parents reasonably expect a range of 'suitable' entertainment for children to be available. The reality may be very different. This is a selection made from film and television listings released during a two-week period over the 'season of goodwill to all men':

Killer Contract
Mortal Combat 2
Recipe for Revenge
Suburban Commando
Shoot to Thrill
The Long Kill
Clubbed to Death
Merchant of Death
Toy Soldiers
Stick Fighting Warriors
Blood on Her Hands

This is a tempting menu for children to sample but does the general viewing public really want à la carte violence? That is doubtful. Some of the most delightful and successful films recently made for TV and the cinema have been non-violent. Broadcasters assert that their programming is dictated by viewing figures; they provide what the public wants. As the BBC states in its commitment to viewers – 'the BBC is what you make it'. It is not enough to argue that children know the difference between factual and fictional violence. All expressions of violence contribute to a climate of acceptance that suggests – particularly to impressionable children – that violence is a normal part of life; violence is entertaining.

Violence – a product of neglect

Children don't invent anti-social behaviour. They learn quickly, are easily influenced and they understandably react to any of the many forms of neglect they may suffer. Schools have procedures for recognising and reporting both suspicion and evidence of serious neglect but, as with signs of violence, much goes unnoticed or is deliberately concealed. Children are given freedoms they are not ready to handle. How many parents of 13-year-old children know, at all times, where they are, whom they are with, how much money they have and what they are doing? The NSPCC estimates that there are between 200,000 and 300,000 homeless children and 53,700 children are looked after by local authorities. We allow children sexual freedom and, in keeping with the times, convey permissive messages. Until only a few years ago, the central theme of sex education in schools was 'family planning', now it is 'safe sex'. To many young minds that change must suggest that, if sex is safe, it is permissible.

For many children, their diet is irregular and unsupervised. Undernourishment, obesity, hyperactivity and many other disorders have been associated with this form of neglect. School catering services cannot reasonably be expected to compensate for a junk-food culture. In one large secondary school, attempts to improve the nutritional value of meals by introducing a 'non-chip day' were met with strong disapproval from students and opposition from a catering service anxious to protect its income. Responding to the needs of many of their students, some schools provide breakfast; though what does that say about a society that sends its children off for the day – unfed – oblivious to whether or not the school can provide? The correlation between truancy and youth offending has been clearly shown and there can be little doubt that there is also a link between truancy and bullying. If educational reform is to continue in the best interests of children and facilitating the work of the school, it must include a review of the professional responsibility held by teachers *in loco parentis*.

Where neglect is concerned, Britain scores particularly well in European league tables. We have the highest divorce rate, the highest number of under-age pregnancies, the highest level of teenage drug abuse, the highest number of runaways from home, the highest proportion of advertising aimed specifically at children and, from the age of 13, our children are the youngest legally allowed to work. It is hardly surprising that, according to the Mental Health Foundation, one fifth of our children have a mental disorder. The Foundation states 'we claim to be a child-centred society but in reality there is little evidence that we are... we are a ruthlessly adult-centred society where children are defined almost exclusively in terms of their impact on adult lives and by governments in terms of their economic potential' (Mental Health Foundation 1999). It is reported that a Danish speaker at an international conference on children and violence, when asked how parents disciplined unruly children without smacking, replied 'in Denmark, we like children'.

Tables – even league tables – can be turned. Much is being done by children's organisations. An alliance of over 200 bodies and many prominent figures has been formed under the banner 'Children are Unbeatable' and there is a vigorous campaign for the appointment of a Children's Rights Commissioner. Reflecting government priorities, the incoming Director General of the BBC placed education at the heart of future developments in broadcasting. On the global stage, the United Nations has declared that 'the years 2001 to 2010 shall be the international decade for a culture of peace and non-violence for the children of the world'.

In dealing with bullying, schools are able to present alternatives to violence and counteract the many damaging influences to which children are subjected. Schools have to be positive places because children are positive and naturally optimistic. Children prefer to be happy and they thrive on success. In the face of criticism and blame, schools must be getting something right. Considering how easy it is to truant, attendance is remarkably high. The DfES figures for authorised and unauthorised absence in England and Wales (for the year 2000/2001) reveal that attendance for primary schools was 93.9% and for secondary schools 90.9% (DfES 2001). Schools provide for the basic human needs of their children: care, shelter, warmth, food, guidance and supervision. This is where children meet their friends, gain new experiences and are released from the constraints of domestic routine and parental control. For many of them, school is a haven from external pressures and deprivation.

Spotlight on the school

It is right that the political and public spotlight should be on schools. Schools have become the cutting edge of a rapidly changing society. They both reflect and serve society but the more schools accept responsibilities on its behalf, the more society relinquishes its own. The messages that teachers routinely receive are a clear indication of this transfer of the duty of care. 'Your children are sitting on my wall.' 'You can do what you like with Karen; I've given up.' 'Why isn't John doing his homework?' 'I can't get Amanda into her uniform.' Every school is unique and there are many ways for schools to achieve their objectives. They can reduce the incidence of bullying and change a culture of anti-social behaviour by determined intervention. Since it is now well understood that bullying persists into adulthood, bullying is better challenged early. If zero tolerance can eliminate vandalism which violates the environment, how much more important it is to reject violence between people. Schools face a difficult dilemma: teachers know that excluding a student equates to rejection and that rejection is psychologically damaging. Rejection is keenly felt by children already in trouble and at risk. They may adopt a bravado stance but they are hurt and they do care. Excluded children might understandably feel like fighting back and return to break a window or send a parent to assault the head teacher.

The strong correlation between exclusion, truancy and anti-social behaviour adds further complication to how schools deal with bullying. Schools have to make a stand on discipline, particularly when it seems that everyone else has given up. The disciplinary principle that most apply is that when an individual cannot or will not conform to the requirements of the school community, then he or she no longer deserves a place there. This is harsh punishment for a child but it is an effective sanction. In the practice of many schools, a clear distinction is made between punishment and correction. If the fault can be corrected, punishment is unnecessary. There is room for flexibility in dealing with individuals but no place for ambiguity. It is for management to establish and sustain a whole-school policy on bullying and ensure that any inconsistency that might jeopardise its effectiveness is avoided. There is, of course, a delicate balance between uniformity of practice and the flexibility that might be necessary in particular, individual cases but the essential ingredient of a prevention strategy is the commitment of the whole school. The introduction to the National Association of Head Teachers' *Guidance on Bullying* (2000) states:

> Bullying is an insidious social problem found in many occupations and walks of life. In the school environment it can be found amongst both the pupils and staff. The role of the head teacher, as manager of the school, is to

11

ensure as far as is reasonably practicable, that structures and procedures embedded in school behaviour policies prevent bullying. Ultimately, it is the responsibility of the whole school community to eradicate bullying by ensuring the development of a caring and supportive ethos.

In spite of the abolition of corporal punishment in state schools in 1986 and in all schools in 1999, an acceptance of violence is still common. On the very last day of the last century, the *Times Educational Supplement* headline on corporal punishment was 'Nation of shopkeepers that knows how to flog', sub-titled 'The British have always been surprisingly keen to make a rod for their own backs' (Wolf 1999).

Suggestions for further action

To initiate and promote a whole-school strategy:

- decide on a launch date
- devise a visual display: posters, badges, notice-boards, etc. (see Appendix 2 'The Charter')
- publicise the plan as widely as possible, both in and out of school
- invite a known personality or celebrity to be 'moral sponsor' or patron for the project
- establish a budget
- invite representatives from local shops and businesses to a presentation of the project in order to gather both general and financial support
- nominate students to be ambassadors to the project.

2 A presentation of *Towards a Non-violent Society – Checkpoints for Schools*

Checkpoints for Schools

Checkpoints for Schools was commissioned by the Forum on Children and Violence, funded by the Calouste Gulbenkian Foundation and launched in 1999 by Charles Clarke, MP, then Minister for Schools. The Forum, set up in 1997, has successfully developed the project in partnership with voluntary, statutory, academic and research organisations. Its work has involved young people's participation and the accumulation of evidence on the use of *Checkpoints*. Workshops for practitioners and young people, conferences and seminars have been organised. *Checkpoints* was launched at a time of increasing public concern in Britain over the prevalence of violence in society. Aggression was seen to be common, anger expressed unashamedly and violence often occurred as the sequel to disagreement. *Checkpoints* is designed for schools addressing their own local needs. It has undergone trials in a wide cross-section of schools and has been revised in the light of feedback from its use. The first publication, *Towards a Non-violent Society – Checkpoints for Schools* (Varnava 2000), was in response to a proposal made by the Commission set up by the Foundation that:

> A series of checklists for working towards a non-violent society should be prepared and disseminated for parents and for all those working with or for families and children, in conjunction with appropriate working groups of practitioners.
>
> (Calouste Gulbenkian Foundation Commission on Children and Violence 1995)

It was decided to start with guidance for schools. Pilot schools taking part in the first trials of *Checkpoints* comment on its use and effectiveness:

> *Checkpoints* has helped to reduce the number of confrontations. It has made us all more aware and keeps us focused. We have established a quiet, secure environment where everyone can learn and feel safe. Even our tough boys now admit to and talk about their problem. *Checkpoints* is working here as a dynamic auditing tool, complementing and supporting other whole-school initiatives. School is not the top priority for families who have to

deal with stress, drugs, marital break-up, prison, etc. Parents only want their children to be safe and happy in school.

> (Head teacher of a primary school in a deprived urban area with 400 students from age 4 to 11)

Checkpoints made a real difference to the student conference. These ideas will form part of a Student Council School Development Plan to run alongside the School's Development Plan. A key part of this will address student safety in school.

> (Head teacher of a multi-ethnic, inner-city secondary school and specialist performing arts college with 1,200 students from age 11 to 18)

I am a member of the Student Council. We have been talking about the safety of the students. I feel that having a Student Councillor is good because the teachers get to hear what students would like to see changed.

> (15-year-old student)

A guide for using *Checkpoints*

Checkpoints is a resource and a process, inviting action on its propositions. It is a self-help tool, neither prescriptive nor judgemental. It has three main functions: to raise awareness, to facilitate institutional self-audit and to offer guidance.

In addition to schools *Checkpoints* can be (and has been) applied to other groups: youth and sports organisations, care homes and early years provision, and, by linking the use of it to other associated groups or schools, its effectiveness can be increased. The young people's version reinforces *Checkpoints* and encourages child–adult and home–school dialogues to take place (see Chapter 5).

Finally, the use of *Checkpoints* leads on to the formulation of assessment criteria by which the school's progress in behaviour management can be measured. Its adoption by other professions demonstrates its adaptability.

Checkpoints consists of a framework representing the main aspects or dimensions of school life. These are:

Home/School/Community
Values
Organisation
Environment
Curriculum
Training.

The scheme is developing in the light of experience, giving clear indications of how it might be used on a wider front. Evidence is being gathered from teachers, trainee-teachers and teaching assistants and, especially valuable, from the observations contributed by young people. Primary schoolchildren, for example, have expressed their fears at transfer stage, anticipating 'bigger children', 'too many people' and 'queuing for dinner'. They expect student behaviour – even their own – 'to get worse' (see Appendix 1 'Discussions with Year 6 students preparing to transfer to secondary school'). They learn quickly which parts of a school are threatening and best avoided. They soon work out – and with precision – a secondary school's 'pressure points'.

Checkpoints for Young People (Varnava 2002), the companion to *Checkpoints for Schools* (Varnava 2000), adds a second dimension to the process of intervention. It engages those who are the object of the strategy and provides the means by which the anti-bullying agenda can reach parents.

Checkpoints – or the seven dimensions of school life

Each of the Checkpoints (on pages 17–29) consist of ten statements relating to different aspects of school life. For Checkpoints 1 to 6, tick one of the boxes: *in place, proposed* or *not in place*. The results can then be transferred to the web (see Chapter 3) to create a visual record. Checkpoint 7 is for schools to record their own initiatives not included in Checkpoints 1 to 6.

Aspects of the learning environment that matter most to teachers

A survey conducted in 2001 with 230 fourth-year trainee-teachers provides information based on their experience in the primary schools where they had done teaching practice. Results show which aspects of the school, as itemised by Checkpoints, were given the highest priority:

- 95% of the students observed that 'creating a happy, non-violent, positive atmosphere is accepted by all as an important aim'.
- 92% of the students observed that 'agreed standards of behaviour apply to all members of the school and to visitors'.
- 92% of the students observed that 'good relationships are consistently fostered and all adults model non-violent behaviour'.
- 84% of the students observed that 'the school helps everyone to adopt a sense of responsibility for one another and for the school'.

To conclude this section here is an observation on *Checkpoints* from a primary teacher in Northern Ireland: 'I think the booklet, as it stands, is a very effective tool for school evaluation and could be used both for staff development and for parent/teacher meetings. I can't think of anything that needs changing.'

Suggestions for further action

To encourage the adoption of an intervention strategy:

– organise a trial run using one section of *Checkpoints*
– arrange to collaborate with another school in planning an anti-violence intervention strategy
– identify ways of raising awareness of the strategy
– draw up a constitution for the School Council or review an existing document (see Appendix 3 'Student Council constitution')
– determine where the strategy can be linked to existing policies.

Checkpoint 1. Home, school and community

A school is a community within a wider community. Like every person within it, a school deserves to be protected, supported and nurtured. Whatever safeguards there are, the school cannot be isolated from the outside world. Parents and the local community play an essential part in the formation of a positive school ethos. Policies promoting non-violence are more effective if parents and the local community are involved in their formulation and development and just as children's home circumstances influence their behaviour at school, so the school can influence children's behaviour outside school.

a in place **b** proposed **c** not in place

	a	b	c
1. The school works closely with parents, providing information and opportunities for discussion, encouraging involvement in the formulation of non-violence and anti-bullying policies.	☐	☐	☐
2. The 'contract' or agreement between home and school includes a specific commitment to non-violence and gives guidance on how parents can help implement the policies at home and at school.	☐	☐	☐
3. Links are made with local community groups and external agencies in respect of violence prevention.	☐	☐	☐
4. The school publicises its commitment through its newsletter and other means.	☐	☐	☐
5. Agreed standards of behaviour apply to all members of the school and to visitors.	☐	☐	☐
6. The school makes it clear that non-violent behaviour is also expected outside school, at home and in the family.	☐	☐	☐
7. Examples of avoidance strategies are presented through the curriculum and promoted in all school policies.	☐	☐	☐
8. The school is clear and consistent in dealing with incidents, particularly those that may amount to criminal offences.	☐	☐	☐
9. The school takes careful note of any circumstances in the local community that might affect any of its students.	☐	☐	☐
10. The local press supports the school in helping to build its reputation as a safe place.	☐	☐	☐

Explanatory notes

1. A structured plan, with the involvement of governors, is made to ensure that regular communication takes place between school and home. Formal meetings, educational and social events form a home–school programme that strengthens liaison for the benefit of individual students and the school as a community. Anti-bullying is included in the agenda of meetings with new parents, general meetings and individual parents' meetings with teachers.

2. A home–school agreement or 'contract', drafted jointly by parents and teachers with the involvement of students and governors, provides an effective reference point if problems arise. The status of the agreement – as part of school policy, local education authority (LEA) regulation or current legislation – is made clear from the outset.

3. Links are made with bodies working in the area of child welfare, including for example, local community safety team, child protection committee, health authority, social services, neighbourhood watch, youth offenders unit, police and youth service.

4. The school publicises itself as a happy, orderly, positive, collaborative place, using regular communication through newsletters, notice-boards and student diaries.

5. Standards are agreed by all teaching and support staff, regularly reviewed, disseminated widely and made visible to students, staff and visitors. Mutual respect and tolerance are promoted.

6. Consistent emphasis is placed on self-control, personal responsibility and self-esteem. In order to help the development of these qualities, all forms of physical and humiliating punishment are prohibited at school and discouraged in the home. Positive discipline is consistently promoted.

7. Students study a variety of contemporary conflict situations, in both personal and social contexts, with action taken to resolve them, for example how a sports referee applies the rules and arbitrates when disagreement occurs. Students are shown everyday examples of conflict resolution. 'Circle time' and school councils play a central part in this learning process.

8. A clear understanding is established of what the school deals with and what it does not. The school calls on relevant agencies as necessary. The whole school community is made aware of the circumstances in which serious incidents – involving either criminal or potentially dangerous activity – will involve the police.

9. Community liaison and information channels are established, for example, through youth clubs, church groups and residents' associations.

10. The school is proactive towards the press, particularly local, providing news, pictures and reports on successes. Working relationships with local education journalists are cultivated.

Checkpoint 2. Values

a in place b proposed c not in place

	a	b	c
1. Creating a happy, friendly atmosphere is accepted by all as an important school aim.	❏	❏	❏
2. All members of the school participate in the development of a Code of Conduct, which specifies non-acceptance of bullying and is made prominent throughout the school.	❏	❏	❏
3. It is understood that the school's values apply both inside and outside school.	❏	❏	❏
4. The school ensures that its rules do not contradict external regulations or laws relating to violence-prevention.	❏	❏	❏
5. Good relationships are consistently fostered and all adults model non-violent behaviour.	❏	❏	❏
6. Mutual respect is consistently promoted and expected of everyone.	❏	❏	❏
7. The school helps everyone to adopt a sense of responsibility for one another and for the school.	❏	❏	❏
8. Violent language, the violent use of language and name-calling are consistently discouraged.	❏	❏	❏
9. All disciplinary measures are unthreatening and appropriate to the individual's stage of personal development.	❏	❏	❏
10. Conciliatory behaviour is noted and commended and assembly is used to promote the values of the school to all its members.	❏	❏	❏

Explanatory notes

1. What most parents want from a school is a place to which they can entrust their children. For many this is as important, if not more important, than the prospect of good academic results.

2. Students, teachers and support staff are all subject to the requirements of the school's Code of Conduct. Their involvement in its construction adds to its effectiveness and facilitates its consistent application.

3. Good citizenship is underpinned by the understanding that bullying or other violence is unacceptable in all circumstances. Students cannot learn too early that conforming to a high standard of behaviour in school is inadequate training if their behaviour outside falls below that standard.

4. In the case of exclusion, for example, additional LEA guidelines may be in place. The school's policy on when to apply statutory regulations needs to be precise and understood by all.

5. Staff training in the use of conflict resolution techniques is essential. Examples set by adults are a powerful lesson to children and serve to reinforce policy and good practice.

6. Disrespect shown by any member of the school or visitor is equally unacceptable and cannot be overlooked or condoned.

7. Many schools have successfully involved students as 'buddies', 'peace-makers' or 'peer counsellors' as part of a strategy encouraging mutual support and promoting a sense of corporate ownership of and pride in the school.

8. Many common words and phrases bring violence into our language. Their use can condition our thinking and imply an acceptance of the normality of violence. An opposing team, for example, is not 'the enemy' and the word 'fight' is used indiscriminately throughout the English language.

9. It is useful for staff to have information on the development of individual students in order for them to match their expectations to physical and emotional maturity. Disciplinary measures avoid physical or psychological harm or humiliation. Exclusion is seen as rejection and must, therefore, be only a last resort.

10. Examples of respect, empathy and other pro-social behaviour are acknowledged and recorded. Masculinity and toughness are not presented or accepted as synonymous; femininity is not associated with weakness.

Checkpoint 3. Organisation

To demonstrate that violence can have no place in a healthy school, it is important for existing policies and procedures to be revised to include reference to non-violence. The anti-bullying policy and procedures are made integral to school organisation, firmly based on whole-school consensus.

a in place **b** proposed **c** not in place

		a	b	c
1.	There is a budget for the implementation of anti-bullying policies.	☐	☐	☐
2.	The induction of new students, teachers, support staff and governors includes the presentation of anti-bullying policies and measures.	☐	☐	☐
3.	The school timetable and daily routines are scrutinised to ensure they do not increase the chances of incidents occurring.	☐	☐	☐
4.	The school ensures that its rules – for example on uniform or releasing students from the classroom – do not become a cause of conflict.	☐	☐	☐
5.	Students regularly discuss violence prevention at Circle time or in a school council, preferably supported by their own budget.	☐	☐	☐
6.	There are student and staff mediators and all members of the school are encouraged to seek help and advice if needed.	☐	☐	☐
7.	Both vulnerable and aggressive students are identified early and support given to pre-empt difficulty. Students themselves and, as appropriate, parents are involved.	☐	☐	☐
8.	A record is kept of incidents and a regular survey of bullying is carried out to complement and reinforce policy.	☐	☐	☐
9.	All members of the school are familiar with emergency procedures, including those relating to visitors or strangers.	☐	☐	☐
10.	All staff know who is the designated person for child protection matters and are familiar with procedures on disclosure and DfES guidance on child protection.	☐	☐	☐

Explanatory notes

1. Policies that benefit from a dedicated budget are more likely to stimulate action, ensure regular review and updating.

2. All new students and staff are briefed on anti-bullying policies and procedures. Note is taken of the scale of both student and staff turnover to ensure that non-violence maintains a consistently high priority throughout the school.

3. The structure of the school day, like the environment or the architecture, can have an effect on student behaviour. For example, close attention to the juxtaposition of activities, length of breaks, time allowed for movement between lessons, accessibility to equipment and belongings can help greatly to eliminate 'pressure points'.

4. Careful scrutiny of policies and rules is an effective means of eliminating anomalies that, in themselves, can lead to disputes or conditions that invite indiscipline. A precise length of tie or skirt, for example, is bound to cause disagreement; firstly, because peer influence is usually stronger than school rules and, secondly, because a rule that aims to establish consistency may be inconsistently applied.

5. Where Circle time or school council is built into the routine, students are more likely to commit to the principles of empathy and respect. The positive and negative effects of peer pressure can be explored and the need to establish norms against violence emphasised.

6. Mediation between staff–student and student–student serves as a framework for developing skills in anger-management and resisting adverse peer pressure.

7. Early warnings of potential difficulty for particular students are acted upon, with the prompt involvement of parents. Support is provided for students with specific learning difficulties and those with a need for personal skills training. All staff are kept informed.

8. All staff note and report incidents of verbal or physical abuse. Records of different types of incident illustrate trends and indicate appropriate action to be taken.

9. Regular checks are made to ensure that emergency procedures are in place, well understood and practised routinely. Security measures, CCTV for example, are only effective with proper monitoring.

10. All staff are required to be alert to signs of abuse and know to whom they report any concerns or suspicions. A designated, trained member of staff is responsible for coordinating action within the institution and liaison with other agencies, including the Area Child Protection Committee.

Checkpoint 4. Environment

a in place b proposed c not in place

	a	b	c
1. Students share in the management of the school environment to reduce the risk of bullying.	☐	☐	☐
2. The premises are kept visually attractive with high quality display that is relevant, well positioned and regularly updated.	☐	☐	☐
3. People movement is free flowing; overcrowding is avoided.	☐	☐	☐
4. Suitable furniture and carpeted areas are provided to allow for cooperative play and social interaction.	☐	☐	☐
5. Buildings, facilities and equipment are treated with respect; litter and vandalism are dealt with promptly to prevent escalation.	☐	☐	☐
6. Temperature, lighting and ventilation are of a suitable standard and regularly checked, creating a comfortable environment conducive to positive attitudes and enjoyable learning.	☐	☐	☐
7. Outdoor spaces have designated social areas, shelter and secure places for cars and bikes.	☐	☐	☐
8. A health and safety risk assessment is carried out, with maintenance completed regularly.	☐	☐	☐
9. Expert advice on security is sought and security measures are installed.	☐	☐	☐
10. There is safe keeping for students' belongings and arrangements for retrieving lost property.	☐	☐	☐

Explanatory notes

1. Students can be involved effectively at all stages, in consultation, monitoring and reporting problems and as members of a 'safe school committee'.

2. The general working environment: colour, light, cleanliness, space, décor and many other factors can affect people's mood. A pleasing environment encourages positive behaviour which, in turn, facilitates learning.

3. Overcrowding can be alleviated by staggered breaks or student guides at strategic points of the premises. Routes through the school are signposted.

4. Noise reduction is an important objective. Carpeting, furnishing and plants enhance the working environment. Furniture appropriate to the age of students is essential. Round dining tables create a more sociable atmosphere than rectangular; chairs avoid the jostling that is likely with benches.

5. Any maintenance work is carried out efficiently. Schoolkeeping staff are centrally involved in shaping policy and procedures that relate to the premises. Sufficient litterbins are provided and students take a positive interest in maintaining high standards.

6. Personal comfort has an important bearing on behaviour, reducing the risk of irritability, protest or aggression.

7. Safe places for children to meet and play, with a variety of resources, are provided. Outdoor spaces have clearly designated areas for sport and physical activities. Car and bike shelters, entrances and exits are well lit.

8. The site is kept clear of potentially dangerous items that might be misused, for example, builders' rubble, metal objects or tools. Health and safety considerations include basic human needs: clean toilets, showers, drinking water and nutritious food.

9. Security devices act as a partial deterrent to violence. Patrols and regular observation can help to give members of the school community confidence in their safety.

10. An efficient system removes temptation and the source of friction and anxiety. Students are strongly advised not to bring valuable or unnecessary possessions into school.

Checkpoint 5. Curriculum

a in place **b** proposed **c** not in place

	a	b	c
1. Non-acceptance of bullying is prominent in the planning and delivery of the curriculum and the school's development plan.	❏	❏	❏
2. Students are taught about bullying, its types and consequences and non-violent alternatives.	❏	❏	❏
3. The issue of bullying is presented in interactive ways and students with different needs and interests are equally involved.	❏	❏	❏
4. Alternatives to violent reactions are demonstrated, for example in physical education and games where emphasis is placed on cooperation and accepting arbitration.	❏	❏	❏
5. A Personal Development Programme focuses on the whole person and the importance of appropriate social behaviour. It emphasises the relationship between rights, responsibilities and duties.	❏	❏	❏
6. Relationships, sex education and parenting skills are an integral part of the curriculum.	❏	❏	❏
7. Extra activities which encourage cooperation are provided to engage students at unsupervised times.	❏	❏	❏
8. Media treatment of violence is studied and critical viewing skills are encouraged.	❏	❏	❏
9. Representatives of outside agencies promoting pro-social behaviour contribute to the curriculum and provide information about help-lines.	❏	❏	❏
10. Specific advice is given on personal safety.	❏	❏	❏

Explanatory notes

1. Non-violence appears in the curriculum in its own right. Class teachers and subject specialists investigate how non-violence can be promoted in their area of the curriculum taking into account the different contexts in which violence is observed and studied.

2. Students are helped to understand what is meant by violence, both physical and non-physical. They learn about different forms of violence, such as bullying, domestic violence, racial hatred, sexual abuse, violence in the media and war.

3. Students learn about violence, not only in an intellectual way but also through role-play, drama and debate. Interactive teaching methods are far more engaging than a lecture. Programmes which rely solely on printed information are usually ineffective because they cannot demonstrate the skills required to deal with violence.

4. Opportunities arise across the curriculum for studying the consequences of violence, for example in history or literature. From these examples, students can formulate alternative, non-violent outcomes.

5. A programme which focuses on each student as an individual and which has a prominent place in the curriculum provides the context in which to foster non-violence in respect of values, attitudes and behaviour.

6. In parenting programmes, students learn about the alternatives to smacking and subsequent benefits for family life.

7. Playground games, physical activities and sports are usually competitive and may involve aggression. Where this is so, there must be control. Losing without anger or resentment is as important as winning without boasting. Key skills, such as problem solving can be developed equally well in football as in chess.

8. All students learn to distinguish between factual and fictional violence, including choreographed violence, realistic fiction, comic violence and real-life violence. Continuing the discussion at home is strongly encouraged.

9. Visiting speakers from organisations which have help-lines explain their services and ensure that students are aware of the assistance available to them.

10. The school considers the need for personal safety training for staff and students.

Checkpoint 6. Training

Regular training for all teaching and support staff is provided to reinforce pro-social behaviour through the curriculum, in policies and in setting examples. Discussion on violence is arranged between staff, students, parents and governors, exploring its causes and effects and why the elimination of bullying is a priority for the school. Induction and in-service training in specific aspects of violence is provided for staff with a designated responsibility and links are formed with other schools and agencies. The following is a list of some of the areas an anti-bullying training programme might include.

a in place **b** proposed **c** not in place

	a	b	c
1. The different types of violence – physical and non-physical, their causes and consequences.	❏	❏	❏
2. Anatomy of an incident: danger signals, involvement, witnessing, the aftermath.	❏	❏	❏
3. Bullying as a through-life phenomenon.	❏	❏	❏
4. The relationship between violence and power, feelings and behaviour, and the value of positive discipline.	❏	❏	❏
5. How changes in children's personal lives can result in changed behaviour.	❏	❏	❏
6. Changing the culture of acceptance of bullying at school and elsewhere.	❏	❏	❏
7. Disagreement, anger, aggression, a push and a shove, violence, revenge: intervention to break the progression from minor to major incident.	❏	❏	❏
8. Problem-solving techniques used to prevent conflict.	❏	❏	❏
9. Being a good listener and a reliable witness.	❏	❏	❏
10. Violence, the law and human rights.	❏	❏	❏

Explanatory notes

1. Staff are made aware of the various manifestations of physical and non-physical violence. They accept that the roots of violent behaviour lie in childhood and recognise the risk factors associated with children developing violent attitudes.

2. Analysis of the constituent parts of an incident provides a useful lesson in how to act effectively to avoid violence. A simple formula to describe the sequence of events: anticipation, behaviour, consequence, is a useful guide to the process of analysis.

3. Bullying in the workplace is an acknowledged problem. It may take the form of unwanted, offensive, humiliating, undermining behaviour towards an individual or groups. Such attacks are typically unpredictable, irrational and discriminatory. They can cause chronic stress and anxiety leading to ill health and mental distress.

4. Analysis of the causes of conflict often reveals a close relationship between power or the desire for it and the use of violence. Separating these two factors helps promote understanding and can guide preventative action.

5. There is a need for information, understanding and sensitivity when dealing with aggressive or violent incidents. It is necessary to know what action can be taken to support a child and change behaviour.

6. Staff understand that violence is a learnt behaviour, that violence invites more severe violence, and that the adverse influence of generation upon generation has to be countered. A community that aspires to non-violence is prepared to challenge and intervene.

7. It is frequently the case that violence occurs as a result of an escalation from resolvable conflict. Role-play is a useful training method for demonstrating this and suggesting how acceptable alternatives to violence can be found.

8. Staff training can be doubly effective when closely related to students' own deliberations. A staff–student common agenda is a powerful tool. In-service training is a valuable opportunity for staff to consider their values, attitudes and expectations and identify ways in which students can be encouraged to confront and resolve difficult matters.

9. Accurate reporting of incidents is a prerequisite of all follow-up action, particularly where official reports or records are required. Giving a description of an unknown person, for example, demands special observation skills.

10. Changes in the law and regulations that apply to teachers and the complex nature of their work require them to review, update and add to their knowledge. Regulations on the restraint of children are particularly important in the context of the school's aim to eliminate violence.

Checkpoint 7. Other initiatives

Every school is unique. Its particular, local circumstances will shape the way it operates. Student conduct and its relevance to the school's ethos and performance will have been addressed in various ways. This concluding 'Checkpoint' invites schools to add any initiatives or practice not covered elsewhere. The following are some of the examples submitted:

	a in place	b proposed
	a	**b**
1. The creation of a 'quiet place' helped to diffuse tension and resolve disputes.	❏	❏
2. Differences between boys and girls – as bullies or victims – were debated.	❏	❏
3. Poetry writing was stimulated by discussions about bullying.	❏	❏
4. *Checkpoints* was used as the basis for a new School Development Plan.	❏	❏
5. Students wrote and published their own 'Charter for non-violence'.	❏	❏
6. *Checkpoints* provided a context for reviewing child protection policy.	❏	❏
7. Trainees on teaching practice became involved in the process and the experience contributed to their academic study.	❏	❏
8. The school advised parents on the time to be spent on homework and a limit on television viewing.	❏	❏
9. The school devoted a term to the theme of 'the human value of non-violence'.	❏	❏
10. The school initiated inter-agency collaboration on anti-bullying, involving the police, social services and local businesses.	❏	❏

3 The Checkpoints web – an institutional self-audit designed for the assessment of current practice and guidance towards further action

Checkpoints for Schools was very interesting and I am happy to say a lot of the positive aspects are already in place in our school. It was a very reassuring read.'

(Teacher from an inner-city special school for 50 students with educational and behavioural difficulties)

Using the web

The web (Figure 3.1) collates information transferred from each of six Checkpoints, making a graphic statement on how far the school has reached in respect of behaviour management and the prevention of bullying. Analysis of the completed web for auditing purposes is uncomplicated and the involvement of students at the earliest stage is an effective way of gaining their commitment to a whole-school anti-bullying campaign.

Aspects of school life in which problems have already been addressed are clearly shown, as are areas where further action is required. The web demonstrates that the strategy is an on-going process, giving clear pointers towards planning and prioritising actions. It is also valuable as additional information for reports on the school's progress for parents, governors, the LEA and the Office for Standards in Education (Ofsted).

The Checkpoints web

The web illustrates six aspects or checkpoints of the school:

1. **Home/school/community**
2. **Values**
3. **Organisation**
4. **Environment**
5. **Curriculum**
6. **Training**

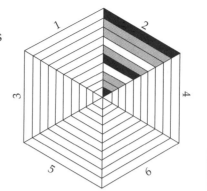

Each Checkpoint has ten statements.

Once the Checkpoint statements have been read and ticked for either: **in place**, **proposed** or **not in place**, transfer the results to the web using the shading key below.

The web illustrates visually the stage reached by the school in addressing violence, and highlights where further action needs to be taken.

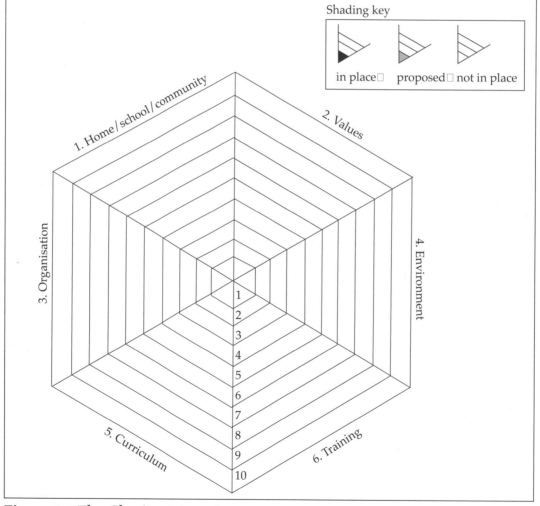

Figure 3.1 The Checkpoints web

Case Study One. Completed web 1 – a secondary school audit

The following example of a completed web (Figure 3.2), with a commentary, is from a large inner-city comprehensive school.

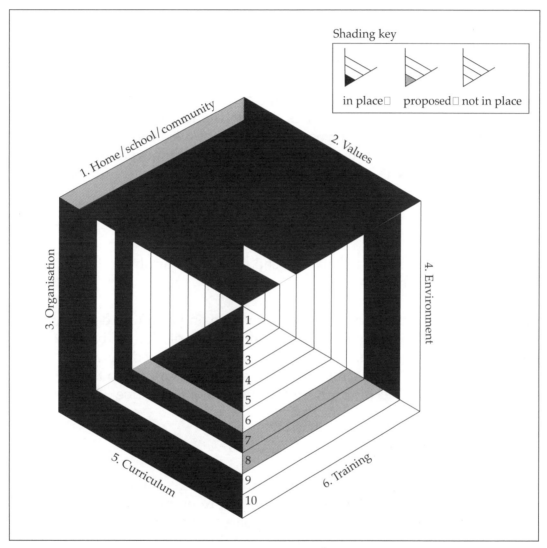

Figure 3.2 Completed web 1 – a secondary school audit

Commentary

Checkpoint 1: Home/School/Community

Item 10. 'The local press supports the school in helping to build its good reputation as a safe place.'

There is a serious difficulty here. The local press regularly covers school activities and – in the case of this school – has concentrated on its problems, sensationalising any incident or parental complaint. The morale and reputation of the school are further damaged. The school works hard to establish new links but, as a result of student misbehaviour in the neighbourhood, the school acquires notoriety and local families refuse to apply for places. The school recognises the urgent need for local support and begins to establish a working relationship with local journalists in order to involve the press in the process of re-establishing local confidence in the school.

Checkpoint 2: Values

Item 3. 'It is understood that the school's values apply both inside and outside school.'

Because of the high proportion of disadvantaged and disaffected students, the school makes a special effort to promote a set of values based on the prerequisites of community life. Its efforts are hampered, however, by its isolation from the local community. This isolation is exploited by some students who – beyond the authority of the school – feel free 'to throw their weight around'.

Checkpoint 3: Organisation

Item 7. 'Vulnerable and aggressive students are identified early and supportive strategies devised to pre-empt difficulty. Students themselves and, as appropriate, parents are involved.'
Item 9. 'All members of the school are familiar with emergency procedures, including those relating to visitors and strangers.'
Item 10. 'All staff know who is the designated person for child protection matters and are familiar with procedures on disclosure and DfES guidance on child protection.'

Due to the level of indiscipline, the priority for staff is a fire-fighting reaction to emergencies. The most urgent matters are treated as top priority but dealing with them is a diversion from other important matters and costly in time and energy. As a direct result, there is little time or inclination to organise the involvement of students in activities that could help to alleviate the problem and assist the smoother running of the school.

Checkpoint 4: Environment

Item 8.   'A health and safety risk assessment is carried out with maintenance completed regularly.'
Item 9.   'Expert advice on security is sought and security measures are installed.'

Concentrating resources on essentials in respect of health, safety and security may be unavoidable but it leaves little time or money for improving the environment.

Checkpoint 5: Curriculum

Item 6.   'Opportunities are provided for students to acquire relationship skills – such as parenting – with an emphasis on non-violence.'

The school plans to include parenting education in its Personal Development Programme. Given that surveys show that the majority of children are physically punished at home, this presents an opportunity to break the cycle of violence that begins in childhood.

Item 8.   'Media treatment of violence is studied and critical viewing skills are encouraged.'

The media's power to engage young people, the lack of control over their viewing and the ease of access to programmes intended for adults are critical issues. It is a disservice to young people not to alert them to the dangers of media conditioning. It is wise, therefore, for a school to include in its curriculum a study of the media, their influence and students' viewing habits. There is understandable resistance to challenging viewing habits and this inhibits productive discussion about factual and fictional violence.

Checkpoint 6: Training

Item 7.   'Halting the progression from disagreement, anger, aggression to violence.'
Item 8.   'Problem-solving techniques used to prevent conflict or violence.'

As the pace of school life accelerates, there is little time available for training, an essential activity that would help alleviate difficulty. The school chooses to start a training programme with the objective of prevention and finding ways of intervening before a minor incident can develop into a serious problem.

Case Study Two. Completed web 2 – a special school audit

The following web (Figure 3.3) is from a *Checkpoints* exercise undertaken at an inner-city special school catering for students with educational and behavioural difficulties.

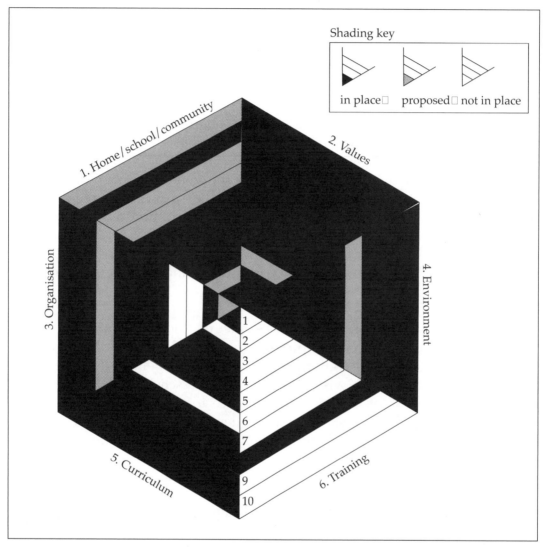

Figure 3.3 Completed web 2 – a special school audit

Commentary

Most of the courses of action advanced by *Checkpoints* are already in place or proposed. The school has clearly considered all areas of the school's functioning in relation to its speciality and the particular needs of its students. However, very little training has taken place, except for staff in respect of conflict or violence prevention. This is an aspect of professional practice for which training is clearly seen, in this school, as essential.

Case Study Three. Completed web 3 – A primary school audit

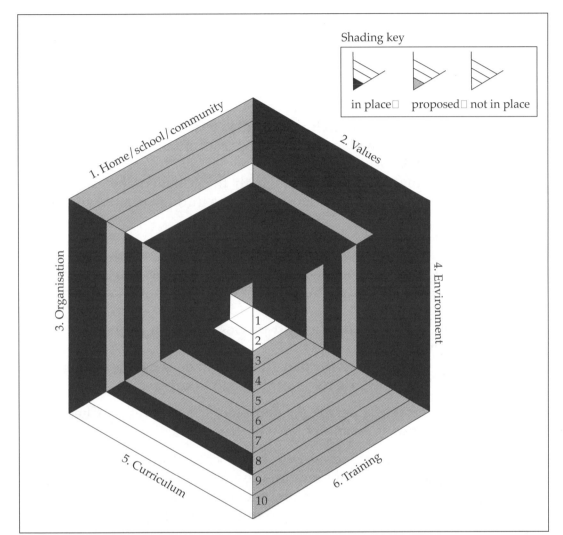

Figure 3.4 Completed web 3 – a primary school audit

The self-audit is a stimulus for whole-school action to address student behaviour. Having completed the auditing exercise, the school reports on the progress it has made.

Commentary

Checkpoint 1: Home, school and community

1. A Home–School Agreement has been put in place.
2. Further in-service work is planned with the LEA and a consultant is to monitor and evaluate our discipline and anti-bullying policies in order to involve parents more.
3. The consultancy is to investigate personal safety issues.

Checkpoint 4: Environment

1. The gardens are flourishing (looked after by staff and children).
2. The school is undergoing a facelift on a rolling programme including improved ventilation.

Checkpoint 5: Curriculum

1. The school has introduced Circle time in all key stages. Staff are undergoing training in Circle time with an experienced teacher in this field, specifically with Years 2 and 3.
2. We are continuing our involvement with the 'Challenging Attitudes to Violence' initiative working on sensitive issues through drama with Year 4.

Checkpoint 7: Other initiatives

1. A 'Quiet place' has been opened. It is already working with children and their families who are under stress, referred by staff and – in some cases – the parents themselves.
2. The school has contributed to a draft proposal to train people as mentors for the children.
3. A proposal to train workers in playground games is in the pipeline. The School Council and the 'H' project continue to flourish.

The school also prepares a detailed action plan, Checkpoint by Checkpoint, from which the following examples have been selected:

- In respect of funding: a budget is to be allocated through the Standards Fund to integrate with equal opportunities development.
- On awareness-raising: ensure staff, members, placements and parent helpers have copies of, understand and implement discipline, anti-bullying and pupil restraint policies.
- For the environment: improve ventilation in classrooms.
- Other initiatives: to train parents as play leaders, through an accredited course to play cooperative games.

Case Study Four. The Student Council

This large, inner-city secondary school holds an annual one-day Student Council Conference, externally funded and held in the City Council House. The conference is an ideal opportunity to engage students from the first stage of the school's strategy to tackle bullying. Student involvement and commitment greatly increase the chances of success. In this case, it is extremely reassuring to the school to note the relevance and accuracy of their observations.

The Principal's letter of invitation stated 'I hope that we can have an interesting and useful morning, and can demonstrate that the Student Council has a key part to play in making the school a safer and happier place with improved facilities for all students.'

The title of the conference was 'Taking practical steps to make the school a safer, happier place with improved facilities' and the conference agenda included an introduction to *Towards a Non-violent Society – Checkpoints for Schools* followed by discussion groups (all ages) using Checkpoints 1 to 5. Each discussion group was to make three recommendations for an OHP presentation in the Council Chamber on the practical steps to make the school a happier, safer place. These would be debated and key recommendations put to the Principal for action.

The Conference report

The Conference report recorded that:

> Each student was given a copy of *Checkpoints*. The Student Council divided into discussion groups, comprising a mix of students across all year groups. A post-16 student facilitated each group. A representative of the funding body explained that the photographs that had been taken during the Council meeting were to be used to encourage students in other schools.

Recommendations on actions to make the school a safer, happier place were as follows:

Group A

(a) Teachers should respect people's feelings and be trained to deal with confrontations and personal issues.
(b) 'Crimes' should be dealt with before they are committed (i.e. prevented).
(c) School buildings should be improved and students made to feel that their possessions are safe in the school.

During the Student Council discussion it was said that special assemblies and so on only occur after there has been an incident (such as a fight) – perhaps they (assemblies) should occur regularly.

Group B

(a) Classrooms should provide an appropriate learning environment.
(b) Theft is an increasingly more serious problem. A place should be organised to keep students' possessions safe.
(c) Measures against bullying should be made clear and apply to all. Teachers should take on more responsibility when it comes to bullying.

During the discussion it was said that: 'many classrooms are stuffy and difficult to learn in'; 'cameras at my old school almost stopped theft completely'; 'we often know who the thieves are – perhaps there should be a confidential staff–student group to which people report'; 'everyone knows who the bullies are'.

Group C

(a) Something should be done about leaving classrooms. Also the lunch queue.
(b) Parents should be made more aware of violence policy.
(c) Praise needs to be subtler as it can sometimes cause bullying.

During the discussion it was said that: 'the individual tutor groups could choose rewards – perhaps applying to the whole group'; 'rewards can make for jealousy – often the same person keeps getting the rewards'; 'rewards should be possible for everyone – there must be something that everyone does that is worth rewarding once throughout the year'.

Group D

(a) Clauses in the home–school agreement should be: open for discussion; enforced efficiently.
(b) Better use of outside visitors – influential visitors should be invited to assemblies and tutor time.
(c) Recognition of achievement – there are many other ways of praising students (e.g. prizes at the end of the year).

During discussion it was said that: staff were looking at different ways of rewarding students, for example, a special meeting at the end of the year to celebrate achievement, to which parents and others might be invited. It may be possible to devise ways of rewarding students such that every student has something recognised (e.g. reward on improvement).

Group E

(a) We should create a stronger sense of community. This would involve: respect for each other; a particular effort to be made in the local area.
(b) We should bring about visual improvement in the school environment.
(c) The Code of Conduct should be restated and re-enforced.

It was said that: there used to be a local community project – one result of this was that students discovered that the community were nice people; a senior member of staff will become a link with the community; the school should rebuild its reputation before asking the community to become more involved.

Group F

(a) Effort should be put into establishing alternative areas on the school site for recreation. More available space would ultimately lead to reduced tension and aggression.
(b) Numbers in the school in the future should be reduced and available space maximised. Everyone should appeal to the City Council. More property and space should be made available.

(c) Sanctions should be applied to violent students – effort should be put into solving long-term problems.

Group G

(a) CCTV systems should be installed: especially in areas where bags are kept; in corridors; some fake cameras could be used; implications of punishments should be very clear.
(b) Refurbishment of some rooms should be undertaken such as new windows and ventilation improvements. Areas such as the lecture theatre provide a nice working environment – which in turn leads to non-violence.
(c) General communication between school and students should be improved: students should be made more aware of policies implemented by the LEA; there should be a central notice-board for students and teachers to see; more confidence should be established in teachers.

During the discussion it was said that it is wrong that the sixth form can't take bags into their area as 'they need to carry lots of things'.

Group H

(a) Communication between students and teachers should be improved – more personal tutors were needed.
(b) Security cameras should be placed in the school, especially in the library, where bags are vulnerable, and in locker areas.
(c) The same ground rules should apply to everyone in school.

During the discussion it was said that: communication could be improved by perhaps arranging 'link-ups' throughout the school between students a year apart; thieving in the school is disgraceful; consistent application of rules should apply to detentions and other things, for example 'some teachers let you chew gum or drink in their lessons, some give detentions if you do'; rules should be the shown on the walls of all classrooms.

Group I

(a) Teaching standards should be brought to a common high standard across the school.
(b) Theft-related crimes are a serious issue within the school community and should be thwarted with CCTVs in crime 'hot spots', such as the male changing rooms and the female changing rooms.
(c) The hard work of the builders on site – in rain and shine – was to be commended.

The Principal closed the meeting by thanking everyone for the excellent contributions and said that the details of the discussions and recommendations had been recorded and would be considered further. Progress would be outlined at the next Student Council meeting.

Suggestions for further action

To strengthen auditing procedures:

- having completed Checkpoint 7 (Other school initiatives), evaluate the measures already taken by the school
- consider the possibility of joint student/staff training
- design an alternative web, diagram or graph to illustrate the school's perception of itself as a community capable of being audited (see Appendix 4 'Alternative display of information for auditing purposes').

4 Establishing base-line assessment criteria for measuring progress

The advantage to the school of choosing its own criteria

Since the inception of Ofsted in 1992 and the political drive towards school improvement, judgements of school performance have been formed very largely by external agencies. These judgements have often been seen by schools as invasive, inadequately informed and unfair. Inspection teams, the media, local communities and politicians have been prompt to offer their opinion, fuelling a general impression that education is at fault. Inevitably, in condemning performance, they also condemn the school. However, natural justice would suggest that the degree to which a school is held accountable for its performance should be matched by the level of autonomy it enjoys.

The completed web is a starting point for the school's own evaluation of progress made over a given period of time. Gaps in the web indicate where action is needed and 'proposed' action is prioritised. The school community itself must agree its aims, set its standards, make its own judgements, be prepared to make its own mistakes and manage the consequences. Where all sectors of the school are involved in self-evaluation, consensus and consistency become more achievable and the school community is strengthened. A sense of belonging and ownership of the process is shared and all members are enabled to participate in shaping their future.

The formulation of assessment criteria is best undertaken by direct reference to the school's own aims and policies. The school's chosen order of priorities for action suggested by the self-audit is the most likely to prove effective. As a first step, nationally determined criteria – such as the number of exclusions – can serve as a convenient and ready-made measure. Although children may be excluded for a variety of offences, a significant proportion of them are removed from the school community as a result of aggressive, threatening or violent behaviour. Exclusion figures are used as an easy way of comparing schools but the essential purpose of self-audit is not to provide data for league tables. The information is much more valuable to the school, having made the assessment, in deciding how best to deploy its resources: material, financial, human and, equally vital, the resource of time. There is much to learn from special schools in this context, where the treatment of indiscipline or bullying is individualised and more time can be spent to support both bully and victim.

Other measures, such as attendance figures, stability of staff, the proportion of lessons covered by supply or temporary staff, test and examination results, can all be taken as indicators of student behaviour. Victims of bullying, for example, often react by finding excuses to stay at home causing a worsening of school attendance figures. The inevitable break in the continuity of their learning puts them at a disadvantage and allows manipulative students to take further advantage of a situation they have created. The explanation given by many teachers leaving the profession is student indiscipline and a high level of occasional staff absence can also result from the persistently disruptive behaviour of some students. The significant increase in the numbers of support staff being appointed by schools suggests that a favourable child/adult ratio can have a positive bearing on the general standard of supervision, student conduct and learning. A second adult in the classroom adds significantly to a teacher's capacity to control. This has been demonstrated in many different situations in both primary and secondary schools. There is a growing number of support staff working in classrooms, among them technical staff, teachers of special educational needs, language assistants, classroom assistants and learning support assistants. More commonly now, the regular teacher is no longer the isolated adult.

A choice of criteria

Schools may prefer to use criteria determined by the LEA or governors, such as the number of complaints made by the public, referral of students to off-site support units or accident reports. Any of these can be a useful measure of the school's general health and well-being. Alternatively, by determining its own criteria, setting its own targets and making judgements for its own purposes, a school retains control of the audit process. This can be far more reassuring and helpful to members of the school community than an audit imposed from outside. The following criteria, employed in a wide variety of circumstances, illustrate some of the ways schools assess standards of behaviour and the school's ability to manage them.

> The cost of vandalism (or, specifically, of broken windows)
> The cost of removing graffiti
> A record of specific types of incident (name-calling, making threats, possession of an offensive weapon)
> A record of injuries
> The number of occasions parents are called in
> The number of times police are involved
> The frequency of detention classes and number of detainees
> Noise levels
> The number of times emergency services are misused: fire alarm, fire hose, etc.
> Attendance at examinations
> The number of times the 'f' word is heard.

Case Study Five. Threat of closure

An inner-city comprehensive school under special measures and threat of closure is criticised by Ofsted, particularly for the prevalence of bullying.

A 'task group' of five, consisting of an experienced Head teacher, an LEA adviser, a seconded deputy head teacher from another inner-city school and the two existing deputy head teachers is set up by the LEA and the Governing Body. It is given two terms to rescue the school and a clear brief:

1. To rebuild pupil, parent, teacher and local confidence in the school.
2. To ensure that serious incidents cannot occur by instituting strong and reliable supervision arrangements.
3. To maintain the current post-inspection Action Plan.
4. To rebuild the morale and unity of the whole staff.
5. To undertake a staff reduction exercise to meet budget targets.

Two months after the 'task group' joined the school the Head teacher reports to the governors:

(a) We have made close contacts and held meetings with a number of outside agencies and organisations: the police, the local Residents' Association, the Greek School, LEA Head Teachers' Association, feeder primary schools, local shops and the local press. The ethos and central purpose of the school are transmitted through these channels and within school at assemblies and by all staff. All communications with the school receive a prompt and positive response.

(b) There is now a high level of staff presence in corridors and at 'pressure points': lunch break, end of school day, school gates, etc. Students who reach the point where they are no longer under the control of the school or refuse to accept the authority of adults are dealt with, ultimately by exclusion. A new secure fence will close off the playing field from the main site, eliminating the 'escape routes' from the perimeter and reducing complaints from local residents. Other breaches will progressively be closed.

(c) All staff are consistently working to Action Plans and the termly Ofsted review visits serve as regular monitoring.

(d) Teaching and support staff show a high level of commitment. A clear objective for all is to build on progress being made. Formal staff meetings have now been scheduled and allow for full discussion and valuable feedback to senior management. There is, I believe, a corporate sense of purpose.

(e) Detailed planning for the next school year is well advanced. Estimates show the need for a significant reduction in spending. This will be achieved partly by 'natural wastage' in staffing and partly by other reductions. Staff are being kept informed.

In summary our approach is twofold. Firstly, managerial and organisational adjustments are being made aimed at eliminating or reducing problems. For example, there is a focus on whole-school policies, action to address matters of health, safety and security, improvements to the physical environment, a review of sanctions and rewards and a clarification of staff responsibilities. Secondly, students' self-confidence and self-esteem are built with publicised expressions of determination, such as:

'I am important.'
'My future is important.'
'If I concentrate on my work I won't have time to get into trouble.'

Measurable improvement was made in the school's overall performance during the two-term involvement of the 'task-group', impacting significantly on the major problem of bullying. The criteria used to measure this progress were chosen as being the most relevant to the school's circumstances at the time and to areas of school performance giving particular cause for concern. They were:

- Percentage of students with five GCSE passes at grades A to C: from 19% to 23%
- Attendance at examinations: 99% (previous figure unavailable)
- KS3 SATs, levels 5 to 7: Maths from 25% to 32%; Science from 30% to 38%
- Exclusions: a reduction of over 50%
- Average weekly referrals to Behaviour Support Unit: from 35 to 15
- Attendance at parents' evenings: from 44% to 77%
- Glazing bill: down by 51%.

Together, these improvements had a positive, morale-boosting effect on the school. Students were kept systematically informed of their progress and successes, involving them fully in the improvement process and giving them confidence in their own ability to succeed. A new school slogan was adopted: 'Every child a champion'.

The school's own assessment of its progress was confirmed by Ofsted's report on the school's Action Plan. Specific improvements and a general transformation of the school's ethos were noted as measured against Ofsted criteria, these being in some cases the same as used by the school.

- Overall, behaviour in lessons has improved since the last monitoring.
- Pupils' conduct in corridors and social spaces of the school has improved.
- Attendance at the school remains above 90 per cent overall.
- The level of exclusions has been reduced.
- The ethos of the school has been improved by endeavouring to instil in pupils a sense of self-worth and by bringing about physical changes to the fabric of the buildings.

On the final day of the school year and the end of the two-term rescue operation, the Head teacher was handed this letter by a Year 7 student.

I know I have not been at school for long but the time I have been here you have been so good to me. And I will miss your talks after school and at the assemblies but I'll miss you. I am sorry you are living.
From Kelly

(Ten out of ten for sentiment; six out of ten for spelling)

Case Study Six. A declaration of intent

This declaration of intent comes from a rural primary school taking a determined whole-school approach to bullying and other forms of violent behaviour.

Working towards a non-violent school

For the duration of the summer term, the staff and the children will be working together on 'the human value of non-violence'. Our definition of violence is as follows:

- the exercise of physical force inflicting injury or damage to a person or people
- the threat of using physical force
- deliberate damage to other people's belongings
- deliberate damage to property
- improper treatment of other people, pushing and shoving, play-fighting, spitting
- improper use of words, swearing, name-calling, spreading rumours
- expressions of great force and severity, shouting at a person or people causing pain or offence, getting into a temper with people
- polluting the environment.

What the school community is going to do as a non-violent society:

- hurt no living thing
- show kindness to animals
- develop thoughts and actions on racial harmony and appreciation of other cultures and religions
- look after people with special needs
- look after people new to the school
- show forgiveness and bear no grudges
- develop an awareness of our environment, local and global.

Teachers, lunchtime supervisors and volunteers from Year 6 will monitor this project and make notes against the criteria. These will be handed in to the Head teacher at the end of each break for analysis and for reference in assemblies. Praise will then be given as well as adverse criticism as a means of improving attitudes and behaviours.

Accentuating the positive

Even in schools experiencing exceptional difficulty, most acts of bullying are carried out by only a small minority of students. Police data, which show that 100,000 persistent offenders are responsible for half of all reported crime, also reflect this reality. The attention and resources the few attract is diverted from the many who can, understandably, feel neglected and become disaffected or resentful. As a result, there is a danger that the whole school community becomes more preoccupied with indiscipline than with pro-social behaviour.

Monitoring indiscipline alone cannot produce a meaningful, balanced view of the general health of the school. The measurement, recording and promotion of good behaviour are equally necessary. The *My Life in School Checklist* (Arora and Thompson 1987) has been used to gauge the extent of bullying behaviour, other types of aggressive behaviour and friendly behaviour in the school at a particular point in time. Praising and publicising success in preventing bullying to the whole school is an effective means of counterbalancing the adverse effect reports of actual bullying may have. For this purpose, good news is more welcome than bad news and better than no news. The prime objective here is to establish a positive working atmosphere, pre-empting difficulties and building the relationships that are the foundation of good learning.

Some examples of 'good news' and incentives used as measures of progress, suggested by participating schools are:

- the 'good work book' – a public record of behaviour celebrated by the school
- awards/rewards given for specific acts of good behaviour (and associated financial cost)
- the number of letters of commendation sent to parents
- the popularity of the school indicated by applications for places
- attendance of parents at educational and social events
- extra privileges awarded.

International comparisons

International comparisons can be misleading since education systems are significantly different. School organisation, starting age, length of day, examination systems, policies on languages, inclusion or exclusion of religious education, segregation, for example, vary considerably from country to country. Similarities between systems, however, are interesting in that they may indicate important or worrying trends affecting the wider international community.

The European Commission 'CONNECT' project 'Tackling violence in schools on a European-wide basis' (2001–2002) has representation from every member state. The project's aim is to augment existing approaches or interventions and consider their applicability on a European-wide basis. Comparisons reveal strong similarities between the content of programmes that have been devised in different countries. For example, schools in the UK will recognise as very familiar the following self-assessment criteria identified by a Norwegian education authority in a school measuring its progress over a period of three years (Gaute Bjornsen personal communication).

1. Number of violent incidents against adult personnel. (Three plus many threats – reduced to none)
2. Number of student injuries caused by violence. (Five reduced to two)
3. Number of incidents involving gang-violence. (Four reduced to none)
4. Exclusions. (Eleven reduced to none)
5. Financial cost of vandalism. (Glass: 120,000 kroner to 5,990 kr.; Painting after tagging (graffiti): 113,000 kr. to 20,000 kr.)
6. Parents' attendance at school events. (From 'very few' to 'most')
7. Figures on recruitment and retention of staff. ('Difficulty' to 'rich variety of applicants')
8. Use of improper or provocative language. (A recognition that language can lead to violence.)
9. Lateness. (Fifteen-minute later start to school day: lateness greatly reduced)
10. Students' evaluation of the school: 'a high degree of satisfaction with the teaching and their school day'. (An essential counterbalance to the assessment made by staff)

This self-assessment exercise gives a clear indication of positive progress measured by the criteria considered by the school itself to be most relevant. As shown by this school, the cost of bullying can be alarming. Financial cost is of concern but the price paid in staff time, disruption to other pupils' work, the lasting effect on the victims of bullying and parental concern are cumulatively damaging to individuals and the school's reputation. Reference to language (item 8) is a timely reminder that the power of language is great. Where that power is used in a situation of disagreement or conflict it can be as hurtful as physical assault. Shouting, name-calling, insult and verbal threats are all precursors to potential aggression or violence, causing personal damage whether or not they are followed by kicks and punches.

In response to a questionnaire circulated to users of *Checkpoints*, the Head teacher of a primary school in South Africa reported, firstly, on whether a base-line assessment was used. The reply was affirmative and measurement showed that:

– the number of incidents of racism decreased, and
– the number of children attending detention classes for bullying-related incidents decreased.

Secondly, to the question 'Did the use of *Checkpoints* influence or change school policies in any way?' the reply was:

– the school introduced a values education programme throughout the school.
– we like to feel that the school has become a more kind and caring place. We would believe that children and staff are more sensitive to and appreciative of the differences among themselves.

Whatever the results of a self-audit might imply about the school's social well-being, the school is also judged by visitors' impressions of its general atmosphere or 'feel'. It is often these unquantifiable factors that make the school's reputation. The approach to the school's entrance, the way one is received, people movement, the absence of tension, the décor, cleanliness, the state of repair, noise levels, smiling faces and purposeful activity give a clear indication of the success of a community. When cautious parents with prospective students report their pleasure and satisfaction in what they have seen, this is an achievement that deserves to be publicised. It will strengthen the school's self-esteem and dispel local myths and exaggerations. The number of exclusions or the state of the toilets may be indicators of where improvements are being made, but what parents, students and staff really want to know is whether the school is orderly, safe, happy and caring.

Suggestions for further action

- Most schools already use specific criteria, matched to their own particular circumstances. It is most useful to map these and start from what is already in place, then devise additional criteria that reflect the school's aims and priorities.
- Some whole-school policies, on sanctions and rewards for example, embody measurable criteria. Publicising successes of different kinds, to include intellectual, physical, attitudinal, can be a positive incentive to others.
- Introduce practical auditing of school progress into appropriate parts of the curriculum. For example, a graph in maths lessons showing the reduction in the number of 'play-fighting' incidents observed in the playground during lunch break.
- Conduct an evaluation of the school using criteria suggested by parents (see Appendix 5 'A parents' checklist').

5 From school to community – how schools take the lead in tackling violence

'Bullying – a guide for parents'

The unintentional ambiguity of this title from a school pamphlet is a reminder of the importance of conveying the right message to the right reader. Bullying is a serious matter and children rightly expect adults to take action to protect them from violence or the fear of it. Underestimating an allegation, or taking no action, conveys to the child that the complaint is trivialised or even ignored. Given the definition of violence adopted in some European countries: 'violence is what the victim believes it to be', the imperative is for a genuinely sympathetic ear. Teachers – in their capacity as carers – become skilled at listening and responding within a framework of procedures understood by every member of the school community. A well-publicised anti-bullying strategy transmits strong, consistent signals reaching out into the wider community. Communication, of course, is a two-way process and messages from children are at least as important as those they are sent. The following poem was written by an 11-year-old girl in her final year at primary school:

> There's this bully at my school
> She bullies everyone
> Even me
> I cry into my pillow every night
> Wishing tomorrow could be different
> I think about the names she has called me
> And what happened when I tried to retaliate
>
> The blood on my pillow symbolises
> Bravery
> My mum would never understand
> I have to lie to stop myself letting out
> What happened to me today.

From the community to the school

Throughout the past decade and a half of educational reform, schools have been under the scrutiny of governors, parents, education authorities, Ofsted and the general public. Their performance, measured by both academic and social criteria and published in league tables, gives scope for commendation or condemnation and, for those schools considered to be failing, the threat of closure. There have been many cases where judgement has been passed with a disregard for the nature of the school's intake, its level of resources and its particular circumstances.

The most serious problems facing schools are not of their own making. Schools cannot be expected to carry alone the responsibility of confronting social ills. Perhaps more than any other organisation, schools work constantly to prevent bullying. They are doing their best to counteract the effect on children of social instability. With the decline or disappearance of supportive structures – the church, the youth service, a stable family and the expectation of a job for life – schools have become 'social hospitals'. Addressing children's varied needs, teachers treat the condition, aim to cure and, attempting more than hospitals, aspire to prevention.

The concept of the community school has spread steadily since early trials established a new focal point for combined learning and social activity. In the 1970s and 1980s, the Programme for Reform in Secondary Education (PRISE) – inspired and led by a number of prominent educationists – campaigned for the creation of schools which, in serving the community, would provide the strongest support for its children. Such schools can no longer be considered experimental; they have become the logical development of an evolving society. In response to the national interest in sport, the arts, the new technologies and lifelong learning, resources are assembled and made accessible for the benefit of children and adults alike. Where children and adults work and play together, the 'generation gap' can be narrowed.

Bullying is a flaw in the fabric of society and damaging to any community. Changing the culture of acceptance of bullying has been hampered by the misconception that the problem is largely a matter for children and schools. The largest teachers' union, the National Union of Teachers (NUT), develops its definition of bullying to show how teachers, too, can be subject to bullying tactics:

> Bullying is a form of harassment in which the bully undermines and belittles or assaults the recipient. Bullies may seek to exploit others' perceived personal weaknesses, either because they enjoy the exercise of such power or because they are under pressure themselves, or even because they believe such behaviour is the best means of managing relationships.
>
> Common examples of bullying include:
>
> – the allocation of additional workload;
> – withholding of work responsibility;
> – changing priorities and objectives unreasonably;
> – the imposition of impractical deadlines;

– excessive and unreasonable supervision;
– unnecessary invoking of disciplinary or capability procedures.

(NUT 1998)

Action taken by schools against bullying can serve as a powerful example to the community, a declaration that bullying will not be condoned. It is equally important to dispel unfounded fears of bullying. The following are two contrasting 'thank you' letters from primary schoolchildren after a pre-visit to their local secondary school – a school with a reputation for bullying.

Dear Mr G
I had a most enjoyable day on Wednesday. I was in Bear group and had a lovely time with Mr P. I would like to say a big enormous thank you to everyone who chipped in to make it a more wonderful day. Your school is much better than I thought it would be. Please have another day like this soon.
Yours gratefully
Katie

Dear Mr G
Thank you for inviting us to your school for the day. I really liked it, especially the basketball and the French. I asked my mum and dad if I could go to your school but they said I couldn't.
Yours sincerely
Joe

A home–school agreement

Action against bullying is strengthened by regular publicity beyond the school walls. In addition to the school's own publications, the local press can add authority to the school's declaration that 'we mean what we say'. An anti-bullying strategy, devised by the school, should reach out into the local community, involving parents, governors, the LEA and others associated with the school. It can benefit from links with community groups, business contacts and the support of the voluntary sector. The most valuable, if not essential, element of an anti-bullying strategy is the collaborative participation of all concerned, particularly parents. Home–school agreements provide a framework for involvement and a commitment to shared responsibility. The following agreement comes from a mixed 11 to 18 school and sports college situated in a rural area, which welcomes students of all abilities and talents and where the emphasis is on the value of the individual.

Home–School Agreement

The school aims to provide a caring community in which the emphasis is firmly fixed on an orderly and disciplined environment which nurtures, in each student, a desire to achieve the maximum academically, physically and personally.

'Valuing Success for All'

The Staff and Governors agree to:

– encourage each student to achieve his/her full potential as a valued member of the school
– aim to become a centre of teaching and learning excellence
– offer a broad and balanced curriculum to meet the needs of the individual
– recognise effort and celebrate success
– provide a safe, stimulating and caring learning environment where each student can flourish
– act *in loco parentis* and monitor students' attendance and punctuality
– offer clear and consistent guidelines on expected standards of behaviour and discipline which will be maintained throughout all aspects of school life
– provide and follow a comprehensive policy on homework
– communicate regularly with parents and students.

Signed: (Form Tutor)

Date:

I, the Student agree to:

– achieve the maximum from the opportunities for learning which are available
– be respectful towards others and be aware of the support activities in the school and the wider community
– cooperate with the staff and accept the rules of the school
– attend school regularly, bringing everything I need wearing full school uniform
– use the Student Planner to record homework, which I will complete on time and to the best of my ability
– remember to get my Student Planner signed weekly by my Form Tutor and Parent/Guardian
– give letters from school to my Parent/Guardian
– respect the grounds, furniture, equipment and books provided by the school.

Signed: (Student)

Date:

I, the Parent/Guardian agree to:

– support and encourage my child's learning at home and at school
– support the school's policy of mutual respect for all members of its community
– ensure that my child attends school regularly, on time, in full school uniform and properly equipped
– notify school with reason for absence by 10.00 a.m.
– be aware of the Behaviour Management Policy and support its rewards and sanctions' procedures
– encourage my child to spend an appropriate amount of time doing homework within a suitable environment
– check and sign the Student Planner each week
– contact the school with relevant information concerning any child
– attend parents' evenings and any other events relevant to my child's education.

Signed: (Parent/Guardian)

Date:

'This *Checkpoints* is for you'

Towards a Non-violent Society – Checkpoints for Young People (Varnava 2002) is a companion to *Checkpoints for Schools* (Varnava 2000). It benefits from lessons learnt from the use of the earlier publication and from helpful observations made by adults and young users. It is designed for students moving from primary to secondary schools but accessible to a wider age-range. It encourages liaison between the two sectors by providing the means for collaboration on matters of mutual interest. A 'Youth Charter for Non-violence' is included, stating the rights that young people themselves feel they should have (see Appendix 2 'The Charter').

As in *Checkpoints for Schools* the booklet gives some facts and alerts the reader to the seriousness and relevance of its content:

– Violence hurts; it can hurt your body and your feelings
– People do not have to be violent: they learn to be violent, usually as a child
– Up to 60 per cent of young people are bullied at some point in time
– Most children at home are smacked
– In 90 per cent of cases when there is violence between adults at home, children see or hear it.

Primarily, *Checkpoints for Young People* engages the students in the process of addressing their concerns. It is a pocket-sized communication with the home, reaching parents at a time when they and their children have many questions about transferring from the familiar climate of the primary school to the uncertainties of a new experience in an apparently impersonal secondary. Questions raised at school are addressed at home and vice versa.

The booklet explains that it aims to draw everyone's attention to the problems of violent behaviour. It suggests what can be done to prevent violence and how the booklet can be used in various ways at home or at school. It informs readers, in accordance with Article 12 of the United Nations (UN) Convention on the Rights of the Child (United Nations 1990), of *'the right to express the views you have and for your views to be listened to in anything that affects you'*. It advises readers: 'You can use *Checkpoints* by yourself, with other people or through the School Council. If you don't know an answer, ask someone at school or at home to help you find out.' Guidance on using the web is given and the reader is invited to make a personal statement, such as 'I aim to be part of a violence-free community.' Students can add their own suggestions in Checkpoint 7.

Towards a non-violent society – Checkpoints for Young People

Checkpoint 1

Home, school and community – In school and out

1. I am involved in making the rules on behaviour.
2. The rules apply to everyone at school, including visitors.
3. I know what happens when rules are broken.
4. The Home–School contract deals with non-violence and suggests how violence can be avoided both in school and out.
5. We work with people from the local community in finding ways to prevent violence.

Checkpoint 2

Values – What we believe in

1. We all want the school to be a safe, happy place.
2. Everyone is expected to show respect for oneself and others.
3. Adults give a good example of non-violent behaviour.
4. Everyone has a say in making the Code of Conduct.
5. We are encouraged to work together.

Checkpoint 3

Organisation – How the school works

1. I know whom to speak to if I am bullied, called names or hurt in any way.
2. Ways of preventing violence are discussed regularly by the School Council.
3. The school spends money to help prevent violence.

4. The rules on behaviour are explained carefully to every newcomer.
5. Other school rules help to support non-violent behaviour.

Checkpoint 4

Environment – Where I work and play

1. My school is a pleasant place and well looked after.
2. I help to look after the school environment.
3. There are comfortable places indoors and outside for me and my friends.
4. Overcrowding on school premises is avoided.
5. There is somewhere for me to keep my belongings safe.

Checkpoint 5

Curriculum – Learning about violence and how to prevent it

1. I learn what causes violence and how I can avoid it.
2. Examples of non-violent behaviour are given, as in sport, where there are rules and a referee.
3. The curriculum covers duties and responsibilities.
4. There are extra activities at breaks and after school.
5. We study examples of violence in TV, video and advertising to help us understand the harm caused by violence.

Checkpoint 6

Training – Putting what I have learnt into practice

1. I know I have the right to give my opinion on any matter that affects me.
2. I explore violence and the consequences of violence through drama and role-play.
3. I learn how to stop anger or a disagreement leading to violence.
4. I understand that adults can be bullies too and that bullying is always wrong.
5. I learn that using violence is never an acceptable way to get what I want.

Checkpoint 7

Other suggestions – What I would like to add

Each student is invited to complete the web as in *Checkpoints for Schools*.

'These are not my children, they are yours'

Teachers complain bitterly that an Ofsted inspection gives no more than a snapshot of their school. *Checkpoints*, in contrast, is a framework within which each dimension of school life is itemised and action is taken systematically under the school's own control. The auditing process is made simple and enhanced by the involvement of students. There are, nevertheless, other aspects of a school less easy to define or use for evaluation. The school's ethos cannot be measured but it is powerfully apparent. Schools with a strong sense of purpose make their educational and social aspirations known widely. Those with a sympathetic understanding of children's needs as they mature make schooling an enjoyable experience. Problems are never ignored and sanctions fit the student rather than the offence; in this way, there is a stronger possibility that a fault can be corrected. An atmosphere in which people relate well and collaborate willingly influences everyone, raising the tone that any observer cannot fail to notice. Where such an atmosphere exists, the school is a stronger and safer community; all members act supportively towards one another and any unfounded condemnation from outside is convincingly repelled. The following letter was written by staff in response to criticism of a school sensationalised in the local press. It says how criticism levelled at a school can be exaggerated or have little bearing on the reality.

> We are ten supervisory assistants at the so-called 'crisis hit' school and are writing in defence of our school in the light of recent press and TV reports which suggest it is beyond salvation, and that bullying and thuggery abound. Some of us have worked here for as long as 14 years and, in our experience, the majority of children are well-behaved, decent and polite, and they do not deserve to walk out through the school gates each day with the label 'thug' hung around their necks. There are some children, however, who have absolutely no respect for authority, who constantly flout the rules and who are determined not to conform. It is obvious, through talking to them, that many of these children have been allowed to do as they like all their lives with little or no intervention from parents or guardians, and yet the blame, allegedly, lies with the teachers. Our teachers are dedicated, professional and as good as can be found anywhere. Many give up their lunch hours to run pupil support groups and provide art, music, drama and language clubs. This is never mentioned in press articles. The school recently took part in a sports and athletics competition against schools from other counties and emerged as overall champions. This, also, is overlooked. Such negative publicity and the branding of children as hopeless cases or lost causes, at a time when many are either sitting exams or beginning work for exams next year is irresponsible.

Society does not treat its children well but there is little point in apportioning blame; social ills result from complex causes and cannot easily be explained by a particular factor. The conditioning that children are subjected to by the media, commercial exploitation, social instability and the overwhelming influence of competitiveness cannot be discounted. Ruthless competition and violence, in a similarly damaging way, have come to dominate what many people think and do. The reaction of many children to the neglect they suffer is a much more likely cause of rivalry, envy, conflict and violence. Insufficient adult time and a lack of care and control can have disastrous results. There is a prevailing attitude that the solution to children's problems can be left to teachers – a transfer of parental responsibility that gives manipulative children the opportunity to play home against school.

Children are not natural bullies or instinctively violent. As with every living species, survival is the prime objective. Many bullies use violence as a means of establishing their place in the pecking order of society, masking their own vulnerability with their dominating tactics. Bullying in schools is damaging to people and institutions alike. Schools do not teach misbehaviour, they are not the cause of truancy, they do not encourage bullying or condone criminality. It is unjust when they are blamed for any of these. In the case of one school condemned because of its students' anti-social behaviour and a public statement made by two local members of parliament that they would not send their own children to that school, the Head teacher publicly declared: 'Remember, this is not my school, it is yours; these are not my children, they are yours.'

Extending the *Checkpoints* approach

Checkpoints is adaptable for organisations other than schools. Early years groups, youth and sports clubs, child care provision and voluntary bodies working in crime prevention, for example, can gain from a custom-made scheme devised to meet their particular needs and circumstances. Prisons, too, which – in popular belief at least – breed violence, would greatly benefit.

Although the focus may initially be on anti-bullying or non-violence, the responsibility for child protection is being supported by the application of a *Checkpoints* process. In the absence of a consistent and coordinated approach, Sport England has adapted *Checkpoints* in a substantial publication entitled *Safeguarding Children in Sport* (2002), acting upon its concern for the general safety and welfare of young athletes. The organisation is aware of a situation in which some individuals use sport as a means to gain access to young people and exploit the opportunity to abuse them. It states 'sport has a duty of care to safeguard all children from harm. All children have a right to protection, and the needs of disabled children and others who may be particularly vulnerable must be taken into account.'

The Child Protection and Safety Unit (CPSU), in a collaborative initiative between Sport England and the NSPCC, has produced a 'starter pack' to help sports clubs develop safeguarding measures by meeting three important objectives:

- children's safety is paramount
- children have the right to be protected from harm
- children have the right to rewarding and enjoyable experiences.

The starter pack's six Checkpoints are:

- Child Protection policy
- Child Protection procedures
- Partnerships

– Education and training
– Practice and behaviour
– Welfare.

Concurrently, the NSPCC has published *First Check – A toolkit for organisations to safeguard children* (2002): 'for any organisation that provides activities or services for children or young people under the age of 18 years'. It states 'children have a right to be safe and happy in the activities that they, or their parents or carers, choose and parents have a right to believe that the organisations to which they entrust their children are safe'. The NSPCC's Checkpoints are:

– Philosophy and principles
– Child protection policies and procedures
– Staff and volunteers
– Partnerships and public relations
– Community and environment.

Alignment of the anti-bullying strategy with the curriculum

Ideally, an anti-bullying programme will involve everyone and permeate the curriculum. As a first step, the programme can complement national initiatives in the areas of PSHE, Citizenship and the National Healthy School Standard, in all of which the theme of safety is prominent. In the House of Lords debate on Children and Young People, Baroness Massey of Darwen, in making reference to *Checkpoints for Young People*, said:

> Guidelines on citizenship and personal education recognise that the school culture and environment are important for the welfare and healthy development of young people; that giving pupils a voice helps them to take responsibility for what happens in school; that teaching styles such as debating, researching and group work are important in giving young people the chance to discuss issues of importance. Also important is personal and social education, which may help young people with self-empowerment, assertion and negotiation skills such as the ability to say 'no' to unwanted behaviour and to seek help. The *Checkpoints for Young People* produced by the National Children's Bureau and the Forum on Children and Violence sets out a youth charter for non-violence, including the right to feel safe, not to be physically or mentally hurt, to respect, to equality and to know that there are people there to help and to be involved in decisions.
>
> What can we do to combat bullying? The Gulbenkian report *Children and Violence* [Calouste Gulbenkian Foundation 1995] called for a whole population approach rather than targeting high risk children or developing punitive approaches. The Forum on Children and Violence has conducted research and helped conferences to debate this issue. Again, the view is that

children's participation in solving the problem is likely to be more effective than draconian measures.

(Hansard 24 April 2002: Column 315)

Extracts from guidance for schools indicating some of the points at which alignment can be made

Personal, Social and Health Education and Citizenship at Key Stages 1 and 2 (QCA 2000a)

Social and moral responsibility. Pupils learning from the very beginning self-confidence and socially and morally responsible behaviour both in and beyond the classroom, towards those in authority and towards each other.

The school environment, relationships and organisation. The personal and social development of children can be enhanced by a school environment that allows them to feel safe and for which they have some responsibility. PSHE and citizenship can provide opportunities for children to become involved in developing proposals for improving the school environment. Social and moral responsibility can be developed through encouraging positive behaviour and relationships, anti-bullying strategies, environmental and recycling projects with local authorities, businesses and the community.

Citizenship at Key Stages 3 and 4 (QCA 2000b)

Our common values require that there are behaviours that we should not tolerate. For example, racism, bullying and cruelty in all its forms are never acceptable.

In the context of confidentiality, matters that might relate to child abuse or domestic violence are also addressed:

Teachers are not able to offer pupils or their parents unconditional confidentiality. If staff receive information about behaviour likely to cause harm to the young person or to others, they must use the school's child protection procedures.

Teachers are not obliged to pass on information about pupils to their parents, although where the teacher believes the pupil to be at moral or physical risk, or in breach of the law, they must ensure that the pupil is aware of the risks and to encourage them to seek support from their parents.

National Healthy School Standard – Getting started (DfEE 1999a)

> Legal requirements. What are the legal requirements your school must fulfil, for example on anti-bullying strategies, smoking policy, road safety, provision of school meals and home–school agreements? This should be well understood and used to inform your school programme.
>
> Involving the whole school community. To succeed, the programme needs involvement from everyone – pupils, staff, parents, governors and partner agencies. Its key messages need to be supported and emphasised in all facets of planning and learning.
>
> The grounds, buildings and rooms should be welcoming and secure. And is that positive, friendly culture echoed in school handouts/publications?
>
> There should be a clear policy and code of practice for dealing with bullying. Devising this and putting it into action, should bring in involvement from the whole school community.
>
> Health and safety should include discussing issues like child protection and domestic violence, within the curriculum.

Permeating non-violent attitudes through the curriculum

Cross-curricular activities aimed at implanting a specific skill or concept have been widely practised, often in response to a perceived educational priority or the supposed absence of a fundamental aspect of learning. Study skills, anti-racism, bilingualism and equal opportunities, for example, have been prominent in this respect. Permeating the whole curriculum, however, with a culture of non-violence is a different process, requiring the exploration of feelings, attitudes and relationships, the focus being more on the person than on the subject area of the curriculum. There is no definitive model for the process of permeation since each school will choose its own priorities and its preferred methods. A school may, for example, select generic principles that have a particular bearing on the prevention of bullying or other violence. These can be presented in a matrix and linked to sections of the curriculum to show the contact points where teachers can introduce each of the principles. Teachers have control of the process, retaining the freedom to develop ideas with the students where and when suitable opportunities arise. The sample matrix in Figure 5.1 indicates possible contact points.

Effective communication is a basic skill for any part of the curriculum to which these principles may apply. Situations requiring negotiation arise constantly. Problem solving is a prominent feature of Maths, Science, Design/Technology and Information/Communications Technology (ICT). Much of religious teaching in the world's many faiths is built on these and

	Negotiation	Problem solving	Sharing	Making choices	Empathy	Self-esteem
English	*				*	*
Maths	*	*	*			
Science		*				
Languages	*				*	
History					*	
Geography						
Des/Tech	*	*		*		
ICT		*		*		
Creative Arts	*					*
PE/Games	*		*		*	*
RE			*	*	*	*

Figure 5.1 The principles/curriculum matrix

similar principles. Elsewhere in the school curriculum, links may seem more tenuous but can be productive, nevertheless. Arithmetical division and team games are about sharing; designing and using a computer are processes in which making choices is an essential first step; in English, Languages, History and PE students learn to empathise with one another and self-esteem is built through literary self-portraiture, pride in bilingualism, creativity and physical ability. There is fertile ground throughout the curriculum for teachers to develop a culture that excludes all forms of inter-personal conflict.

Widening the curricular debate – a view from the outside

In practice, schools do have a degree of autonomy in constructing a whole curriculum, building on the National Curriculum with what is considered to be most relevant to their particular needs. Where student behaviour is of concern because it inhibits learning, the curriculum can be honed as an effective tool to shape pro-social behaviour. Although new reforms often seem prescriptive, the requirement to innovate is an opportunity to review existing provision and formulate strategic development. In spite of occasional government assurances on a relaxation of curricular reform – even offering a promise of a 'five-year moratorium' – schools cannot stand still. Curriculum does, after all, mean 'a racing chariot'.

Teacher unions, specialist associations and others systematically contribute to the education debate maintaining a flow of opinion and advice directed at political decision-makers. The intensity of educational reform over the past decade and a half, moreover, has increasingly attracted the attention of other professions and organisations. Coming from a wide and varied field, acknowledging the importance of education to them, these bodies have contributed to the debate. Added to the DfEE's own *All Our Futures* (1999b), The Calouste Gulbenkian Foundation's *Passport – A framework for personal and social development* (2000) and the creation of *Centres for Curiosity and Imagination* (Kids' Club Network 2000) are striking examples of different perceptions of how young people learn and take up their place in society. There is a powerful movement towards the provision and development of learning opportunities outside the traditional framework of schools. Commerce depends on entrepreneurial talent, industry demands a skilled workforce and public services are striving for higher standards and adequate recruitment to make improvement possible. Together, these interests reflect a national desire for an effective education service, a desire voiced on behalf of the nation by Tony Blair, the incoming Prime Minister in 1997 as his government's mission statement 'education, education, education'.

The Royal Society of Arts (RSA) joined the debate with its publication of *Opening Minds – Education for the 21st century* (Bayliss 1999). This mirrored an influential development in Quebec, Canada in 2000, described as a 'competency-based approach which will allow teachers to differentiate between students' needs and tailor instruction to individual needs by using students' real interests'. The RSA report argues for a redefinition of the curriculum and a re-structuring of education around a new, competence-led curriculum. It observes:

> The practical challenges faced by education are not simply economic. In many countries, Britain among them, rising prosperity has been accompanied by substantial social change, some of it problematical: family breakdown, changing attitudes to personal relationships, social exclusion. More generally, young people face an increasingly complex world where many old certainties have disappeared. The effects of these developments are very quickly felt in schools. They are places which often seem to bring together and focus the challenges posed by economic and social change. But the ability of schools to cope with the impact of these changes beyond their boundaries is in question. This is true in both the economic sphere – as expressed by the rising number of employers engaged in what they openly refer to as 'remedial education' of their new recruits fresh from school or university – and the social, as expressed in the view that schools are failing to educate young people to function in democratic society.

Taking a radical view of a curriculum undergoing accelerating change, benefiting from new technologies, affluence and globalisation, the RSA points to the particular relevance of student behaviour. There is a sensitive balance between the dependence upon intellectual criteria for evaluation and the importance of personal relationships as the foundation of effective learning. Young people's attitudes towards one another, their corresponding behaviour and their personal commitment to learning are fundamental to their success or failure and how they are judged. A 'democratic society' is one in which we treat one another equally and well.

Suggestions for further action

To establish the school as a focal point of the community:

- nominate one or more 'link persons' to liaise with external groups to include, for example, local shops, supermarket, youth groups, church, bus station, police, residents' association, local press
- write an article or letter for the local press, preferably with the students (for example see Appendix 6 'Letter to the press')
- draw up a 'principles/curriculum' matrix (see Figure 5.1)
- involving students, adapt the home–school agreement in this chapter, adding or amending to suit local circumstances
- discuss with students Article 12 of the UN Convention (United Nations 1990):

    Parties shall assure to the child who is capable of forming his or her own views the right to express those views freely in all matters affecting the child, the views of the child being given due weight in accordance with the age and maturity of the child. For this purpose, the child shall in particular be provided the opportunity to be heard in any judicial and administrative proceedings affecting the child, either directly, or through a representative or an appropriate body, in a manner consistent with the procedural rules of national law.

- The Children and Young People's Unit set up in 2000 aims to establish a children's perspective in government. Discuss with students how their voice can be heard by policy makers.

6 Training – the professional development of staff and the personal development of students

The need for training

Behaviour management, including approaches to dealing with bullying, is now generally included in the initial training of teachers and in the newer courses created for teaching assistants. For trainees preparing to enter teaching, one of the areas of greatest concern is the management of behaviour. They will need to create the right kind of learning environment and develop the working relationships necessary to sustain confidence and motivation for learning for the individual and the group.

As the accumulation of new reforms places greater demands on teachers, the introduction of in-service education and training (INSET) days becomes inevitable. Training is costly, time-consuming and – if teachers or support staff are withdrawn from normal duties – another price to pay is the discontinuity in students' learning and supervision. However, it is unreasonable to expect training to be added to a normal school timetable. Training is a vital part of any whole-school plan to address the ever-present issue of bullying. To be effective in the long term, training to counteract bullying must also be continuous.

Training not only informs but also:

– is the opportunity to evaluate policy and practice
– helps to establish a common understanding of the nature and scale of an issue
– encourages consensus on dealing with problems and plans of action
– explores ways in which the non-acceptance of bullying can permeate school life
– confirms the need to take action
– determines who does what when.

Although an external consultant/trainer can deliver an objective assessment of the school's needs, an in-house training programme has many advantages. Bullying is a sensitive matter; within every school community it is likely that there are both child and adult bullies, child and adult victims. Awareness-raising can help to reduce the problem but training sessions provide an opportunity for everyone to become self-aware, build sound working relationships and share a commitment to the elimination of bullying.

For a variety of reasons, many schools are experiencing significant staff changes; in some cases, there is a comparable mid-year turnover of students. This, in itself, presents the need for regular and repeated training. With a changing population, it is important to note that often the 'newcomer' or someone who 'doesn't fit' becomes a victim or – in order to establish his or her position in the school's hierarchy – becomes a bully. Induction of all students and staff needs to be systematically provided and reflect the school's values, demonstrating that bullying is unacceptable.

The *Checkpoints* training agenda

Checkpoint 6 in *Checkpoints for Schools* (Varnava 2000) and Checkpoint 6 in *Checkpoints for Young People* (Varnava 2002) are agendas for training. If the staff agenda and the student agenda are directly related, consensus and consistency are more likely to be achieved. The following aspects of violence concern both students and staff and serve as useful themes for training and a starting point for discussion or role-play:

Example 1 from *Checkpoints for Schools*

Checkpoint 6, Item 10. 'Violence, the law and human rights'.

The prohibition of physical assault in schools and the authority given to teachers to use 'reasonable force' are conflicting regulations. They allow the possibility of complaint or legal dispute. Physical contact is often interpreted differently by the parties involved and damaging accusations follow. In such cases – at least in terms of reputation or career – the student has little to lose and the teacher has everything to lose. This does not make arbitration easy. There is a serious dilemma for the teacher: he or she carries the responsibility for maintaining order, would naturally wish to prevent injury and has to contend with the disruptive student's challenge: 'you can't touch me'. There is an opportunity here, through role-play, to explore the process of arbitration.

Example 2 from *Checkpoints for Young People*

Checkpoint 6, Item 5. 'I learn that using violence is never an acceptable way to get what I want'.

The difficulty in advocating non-violence is that violence works, at least in the short term. Children learn from an early age that smacking is how parents get what they want. Corporal punishment has been abolished in schools but not in the home. All forms of physical assault, including smacking, have been totally banned in a number of European countries. Smacking is part of the cycle of violence that is handed down from generation to generation. Children who are smacked learn that violence is an effective form of discipline; they too are likely to resort to violence. Smacking children is not normally included in the category of domestic violence yet it is clearly the commonest form. The Metropolitan Police Service (MPS) follows the Association of Chief Officers of Police definition of domestic violence: 'Any incident of threatening behaviour, violence, or abuse (psychological, physical, sexual, financial or emotional) between adults who are or have been intimate partners or family members, regardless of gender.' The NSPCC finds that in 90% of domestic violence cases, children are in the same or next room where the incident took place. The psychological harm children can suffer in these situations is immeasurable. This would be a valuable if sensitive topic for a parent/teacher open debate, led – in the interests of diplomacy – by a visiting expert.

Example 3 from *Checkpoints for Schools*

Checkpoint 6, Item 6. 'Changing the culture of acceptance of bullying at school and elsewhere'.

Peer pressure is commonly given as an excuse for indiscipline, anti-social behaviour, crime, and the abuse of drugs, alcohol or tobacco. Influence, of course, can be applied for good or ill. A relevant example comes from a survey of smoking among students of a large secondary girls' school, which showed that most gave as the reason they began smoking was 'because of friends' and most of those who gave up smoking asserted that they also did so 'because of friends'. A question school staff might fruitfully explore is whether or not there are differences between boys and girls in their susceptibility to peer pressure and the degree to which each is victim or perpetrator of violence. The Economic and Social Research Council (ESRC) key findings in *A View from the Girls: Exploring violence and violent behaviour* (2002) illustrate the scale of bullying and violence:

- 98.5% of girls had witnessed at first hand some form of inter-personal physical violence
- 58% reported being worried about being sexually attacked
- 41% had experienced someone deliberately hitting, punching, or kicking them
- 91% reported receiving verbal abuse
- 10% described themselves as 'violent'.

Practical suggestions for effective training

Education is subjected to incessant change and innovation. In response, training is essential but training in ever-present matters such as behaviour management, is often low in the order of priorities. Time and other resources are directed towards day-to-day matters and little remains that can be invested in improving the working climate and preparing for the future. If schools are to undertake such training in addition to the considerable demands made on them it is vital that training is relevant and cost-effective. Trainers and facilitators vary greatly in their approach. An 'in-house' facilitator is likely to conduct a session in a different way from a visitor: each has a different starting point. Although the subject of training programmes and their aims will be predetermined, a few simple practical measures can help to ensure that sessions are both effective and pleasurable.

A practical guide to the delivery of staff training

Style

- Consider the 'personal stamp' – appearance, voice and how one is introduced – these give a strong first impression.
- An open, approachable manner is appropriate: teachers prefer to be treated as professionals rather than students.
- Determine a suitable level of formality / informality.
- Greet and welcome participants.
- Keep a sense of humour.
- Be prepared to include 'moments of silence', to encourage reflection.
- Visit but don't take over group discussions.

Methodology

- Establish confidentiality.
- Vary the approach and resources, e.g. 'ice-breaker', input, group-work, role-play, brainstorming, debate.
- Value contributions made by participants.
- Give each working group a different task or topic.
- Be prepared to adjust in the light of trainees' responses.

Venue

- If at school, avoid the staff-room.
- Ensure that the ambiance is conducive to collaborative learning: heating, light, comfort, seating arrangement.
- Provide a good visual effect: flowers, display, etc.
- Confirm catering arrangements.
- Move to a separate space for lunch.

Content

- Ensure quality of resources, particularly projected and printed material.
- State aims in advance.
- Find out about participants: number, composition, current concerns.

Timing

- Announce start and finish times and keep to them.
- Time each section of the programme.
- Avoid spending more time than necessary on any section.
- Suggest follow-up activities.
- Propose timetable for future training.

Organisation

- Liaise with school organiser or link person.
- Agree all details.
- Get names of key staff involved.
- Confirm availability of venue, equipment and resources.
- Have an 'emergency box' of resources and spare hand-outs.
- Invite a volunteer to be 'rapporteur' at start of group-work session.
- Remember the wise teacher's rule: 'Never get between the children and their food!'

Evaluation

- This is essential for the planning of subsequent training.
- Keep it simple, focused and relevant.
- Allow time for verbal feedback.
- Review own performance as a trainer.

A sample framework for an INSET day

Effective in-service training is tailored to the particular needs of the school for all teaching and support staff and, if possible, representatives of parents, governors and students.

Aims:

- to reach consensus on what constitutes 'unacceptable behaviour'
- to agree on a unified approach to dealing with it
- to translate policy into action.

Programme

Session 1

Input: An overview – children and the prevalence of violence in society.

Activity: Discussion in pairs. What is bullying? Report back with one statement per pair. Display these for the whole group.

Session 2

Input: Presentation of *Checkpoints for Schools*.

Activity: Group-work. Each group of four works through one 'Checkpoint' and completes the relevant section of the web. Each group reports, the web is completed and displayed to initiate debate on its implications.

Lunch

Session 3

Input: Identification of the 'pressure points' in the school day: time, location, congestion, particular change-over of lessons, etc.

Activity: Participants re-group differently from before and each group takes a section of the school 'time-line', i.e.

> Before school
> First teaching session
> Morning break
> Second teaching session
> Lunch break
> Third teaching session
> After school.

In the context of this 'time-line' and from experience, each group identifies the kind of incident that might occur and agrees on appropriate action.

Plenary session

A school action plan: who does what when?

Training for school students

Anti-bullying training is as important for students as for staff. It includes students in the formulation of policy and encourages them to contribute to a positive ethos from which everyone can benefit. In the light of their experience of involving students, many schools have developed peer support schemes and peer counselling schemes. These have been a significant factor in achieving improvement in general standards of behaviour. School life provides ample opportunity for the promotion of non-violent attitudes and behaviour through the curriculum, daily routines, and personal relationships but specific training cannot be left to chance. Checkpoint 6 in *Checkpoints for Young People* offers suitable topics and Case Study Four in Chapter 3 is an excellent example of effective training, with the process largely in the hands of the students themselves.

Throughout the primary and secondary sectors there are particular points in time when training is particularly appropriate. As students join their new school, it is essential for their induction to include reference to the non-acceptance of bullying or any other form of violence. Also, collaboration between primary and secondary schools at the point of transfer ensures that students are well prepared and understand the expectations made of them by their new school.

Sound, positive relationships – among students and between students and staff – are the foundation of effective learning and pro-social behaviour. The class teacher and the form tutor have a daily opportunity to guide and develop these relationships and assembly is the occasion when clear, unambiguous, keynote messages are transmitted to the whole school community: there can be no doubt about what is expected of everyone. PSHE and Citizenship – both concerned with the personal development from 'self' to 'society' – are most likely to include aspects of personal conduct. Other parts of the curriculum are also susceptible to pro-social training. Physical education and sport, for example, demonstrate the necessity of abiding by rules and accepting arbitration. Drama, too, is a very effective means of exploring the nature of bullying, its consequences and methods of avoiding it.

Topics for discussion and debate

The following topics, initiated by newspaper headlines, are suitable for discussion and debate with students or staff.

– Life of violence can be predicted at age three.
– School's violence culture condemned.
– Swat squad of teachers sent to tame school from hell.
– More young children watching TV violence after 9 p.m. watershed.
– Offer help not expulsion.
– Germany attacks Britain's use of child soldiers.
– Security in playtime patrols.
– Staff underestimate how much they can improve behaviour.
– Bullying rife in Britain's caring jobs.
– Bullies force dad to move son from harm's way.
– Martial arts therapy for troubled teenagers.
– Exclusion 'promotes bad behaviour'.
– Truancy drive on the buses.

Other ways to stimulate discussion can be to:

– investigate an actual incident with the students involved, analysing the cause, the way the incident developed and the consequences. Identify points at which conflict could have been avoided
– record in detail the events of a typical, or untypical, school day and consider whether any particular circumstances may have had a bearing on behaviour (see Appendix 7 'A typical day')

- review the school's anti-bullying policy
- establish a consensus on the meaning of 'reasonable force'.

Suggestions for activities in Circle time or Student Council

Possible activities for use in Circle time or Student Council are:

- discuss and compare our fears
- compile a list of violent words and phrases used metaphorically and suggest alternatives. For example, 'take a stab at it' – try
- discuss what is and what is not bullying. For example, being ridiculed, being humiliated, being ignored, being excluded from a group, being the object of rumour, unwanted attention or contact
- discuss the dilemma of 'to tell or not to tell'
- ensure that the outcomes of these activities are fed into the school's planning and policy-making and reported to parents and governors.

7 Conclusion

'We need action, now!'

The appeal for action made by Louise in the introduction to this book has inspired the continuing development and dissemination of *Checkpoints* – an intervention strategy to tackle bullying that takes a sure step towards prevention. This book is a record of how that process has evolved and it describes, in situations where behaviour has become an issue, how the children and adults of the school community have done something about it themselves.

In the high-profile debate on socially destructive behaviour, facile comparisons between schools or systems do not guarantee that action is taken. Only a systematic, local effort is capable of matching a solution to the problem. Whatever success individual schools achieve, the national objective must be a sea-change of attitudes and behaviour across society as a whole: an essential step on the route to global harmony. The survival of the planet depends on it. Teachers have the skills to lead an anti-violence movement and schools can provide the framework in which action can be taken. With external support, their chances of success – for their own members and potentially for the wider community – improve greatly.

The largest pool of potential support is the voluntary sector. In England and Wales in 2002, according to the Charities Commission, there are 185,000 registered charities, a great many of them dealing with children and young people. These are run by over 1,000,000 trustees (although for all charities there are estimated to be about 3,000,000) giving their time and expertise to worthwhile causes. The registered charities have a combined income of £25 billion and assets amounting to more than £60 billion (Charity Commission 2002). Integrated action taken by education and the voluntary sectors would dramatically increase the attention, care, guidance and influence so obviously needed by a significant proportion of children and young people.

We can't blame children for being anti-social. Blame is irrelevant. They have learned to misbehave by following example, when correction is absent or if their needs are not met. Children are not born violent but they are natural-born learners and they learn mostly from adults, lessons both good and bad. Unfortunately, the flow of influence between children and adults is not always mutually beneficial. However, the nature of schools does encourage and facilitate the kind of negotiation between adults and young people that is necessary when a community is seeking to improve and grow. In this respect, schools set an example to the wider community by rejecting the kinds of behaviour that many adults appear to accept as normal. The public display of these norms, at home, in the street, throughout the fabric of society, put under the spotlight by the media, cannot but influence the young. Anti-social behaviour has become fashionable; violence has become entertaining. The effect on impressionable children is pernicious. It is time to influence the influential.

A society will always need schools even if they are called by a different name. As far as anyone can foresee or hope for, the school of the future will be a community prized within the wider community. It will be generously funded and, like its members, will be nurtured, encouraged and supported. It will value progress as highly as achievement and collaboration above competition. It will reject facile judgements of people, practice or performance. Its material resources will be sophisticated, complementing highly trained teachers. It will be controlled by suitably prepared managers and constructively monitored with expertise, experience and understanding. It will celebrate success and will redress – not condemn – failure, recognising that education is a means to amend. Its mission will be to preserve the dignity of the individual and guide the personal development of every member in a climate of positive relationships. There will be no bullying.

Appendix 1
Discussions with Year 6 students preparing to transfer to secondary school

This is a report on discussions with two groups of Year 6 students preparing to transfer to secondary school.

Group A

Some students anticipated swearing and racist comments, believing that these would be more common than in their primary school. They also assumed that punishments would be harsher. In large premises and grounds, there would probably be hidden corners or spaces where 'bullying could take place in secret'. Bullying would come from older students and fights might occur between students from different primary schools. They were frightened to tell, thinking that they would be seen as 'tell-tale', although fear of repercussions was strongly hinted at. Girls, in particular, were concerned that they 'might not fit in'. They thought that, generally, their own behaviour might change in order for them to be accepted but they also assumed that teachers would be stricter. They believed that they would not get away with things so easily, although they were reluctant to give examples of their likely misdemeanours other than 'not handing in homework' and 'messing about in class'. They felt it would be helpful, at first, to get to know their form tutor well: this would help them settle. Some were unsure about the different teaching styles they would meet. Commenting on their recent visit to the secondary school, some were positive and reported on the pleasant way they had been spoken to by the secondary students.

Group B

Their first fears were of not being able to find their way around, meeting bigger children, bullying, not being able to keep up with schoolwork or homework and other students demanding money. One student confidently predicted that 'we will get more naughty'. Others added their expectation of peer pressure and how it was going to be easier to be naughty because of the premises being spread out. They were 'going to be cheeky, shouting and throwing things'. The boys wanted to impress the girls so badly, they thought loud behaviour would become normal. They thought the secondary school was going to be stricter but their older brothers and sisters had told them this was not the case. On the question of schoolwork, they were hoping to get help from their parents during the summer break.

Appendix 2
The Charter

Visual display of the school's non-violence campaign is an effective means of ensuring that important messages reach all concerned. 'The Charter' was written and designed as a poster by children and young people from all over England. Workshops were coordinated by the Forum on Children and Violence in the summer of 2001. The Charter was developed in partnership with Young National Children's Bureau, the Conflict Resolution in Schools Project (CRISP) and the Woodcraft Folk's International summer camp.

Violence is not the right solution – a youth charter for non-violence.

We have the right:

- to be and feel safe
- not to be physically or mentally hurt
- to a good education
- not to be bullied
- to respect
- to equality
- to be involved in decisions that affect us
- to speak for ourselves
- to know that there are people there to help
- to a say in running our schools.

2001 to 2010 is the United Nations Decade for a Culture of Peace for the Children of the World. In each year of the decade the Forum will be working with young people to develop practical solutions that will make society a safer place for them.

Appendix 3
Student Council constitution

Awareness-raising among all members of the school community is the essential first aim of a violence prevention strategy. A guiding principle for the development of the strategy is that involvement is as important as communication. Opportunities for staff, parents and governors to discuss the strategy may already exist routinely but, unless students are given similar opportunities, their opinions cannot be taken into account and students are less likely to become involved. The School, or Student, Council has become the most widely adopted arrangement for student participation and a constitution establishes its legitimacy, purpose and continuity. The following is an example of a secondary school constitution.

School Council constitution

Aims

- to foster good relationships within the school
- to use the school's resources in the most effective way
- to encourage the expression of students' views
- to promote discussion between students and between students and staff
- to ensure that every student understands the working of the school
- to support the Head teacher and staff in making the school a place of learning for the benefit of everyone

Membership

- two class representatives elected by the class (These form the Full School Council.)
- two year representatives elected by each Year Council (These form the Executive Committee.)
- committee Officers: Chairperson, Vice-chairperson, Secretary, Treasurer, elected by the Executive Committee, at least one Officer to be a senior student

Links through personal representation

These will be made between the School Council and:

– Sixth Form Committee
– The School Association (Parent–Teacher)
– Governors of the school
– Head teacher and staff

Meetings

– one Year Council meeting at least for each Year, every half-term
– one Full School Council meeting at least every half-term
– one Executive Committee meeting at least every half-term

Appendix 4
Alternative display of information for auditing purposes

The *Checkpoints* web is a visual device giving a composite picture of the range of measures used to tackle a particular problem – in this case, violence or, specifically, bullying. The web is one of many possible models. The hexagonal diagram can be used with different rubrics but there are many other graphic ways of displaying information gathered from the various areas of enquiry. Any relationship detected between the measures taken and the time, location or frequency of incidents occurring will indicate where intervention is required.

Actions taken or proposed for preventing incidents taking place at the 'pressure points' that have been identified at particular times of the day and in certain locations can be plotted along a simple 'time-line' dividing the day into sessions (Figure A4.1). An analysis of where and when incidents occur may indicate whether or not there is a tendency for these to be linked in any way to particular aspects of organisation. Are most reports of bullying, for example, from younger students being jostled in the lunch queue?

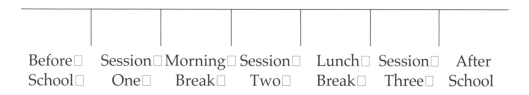

Before☐   Session☐ Morning☐ Session☐   Lunch☐ Session☐   After
School☐   One☐   Break☐   Two☐   Break☐   Three☐   School

Figure A4.1 The time-line – an analysis of institutional 'pressure points' of time and location

Actions taken or proposed by the school to connect with the local community, maintaining good communications, building support and conveying a sense of community ownership of the school can be represented using a concentric model with the school at its centre. This illustrates the points of contact and the relationships between the school, its locality and its supporters (Figure A4.2).

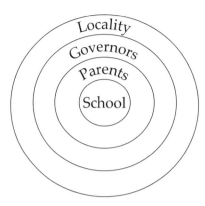

Figure A4.2 The school and the community – plotting the links and relationships

Actions taken or proposed in relation to whole-school policies can be represented using a web similar to that used for *Checkpoints* (Figure A4.3). This approach assists the school in maintaining coherence between policy and practice. For example:

Health and safety	–	Immediate removal of builders' rubble
Equal opportunities	–	Separate record of racist incidents
Sanctions and rewards	–	Regular celebration of success
Home–school contact	–	Procedure for tracking latecomers
Homework	–	Timetable sent to parents
Assessment of students	–	Correlated with behaviour measures

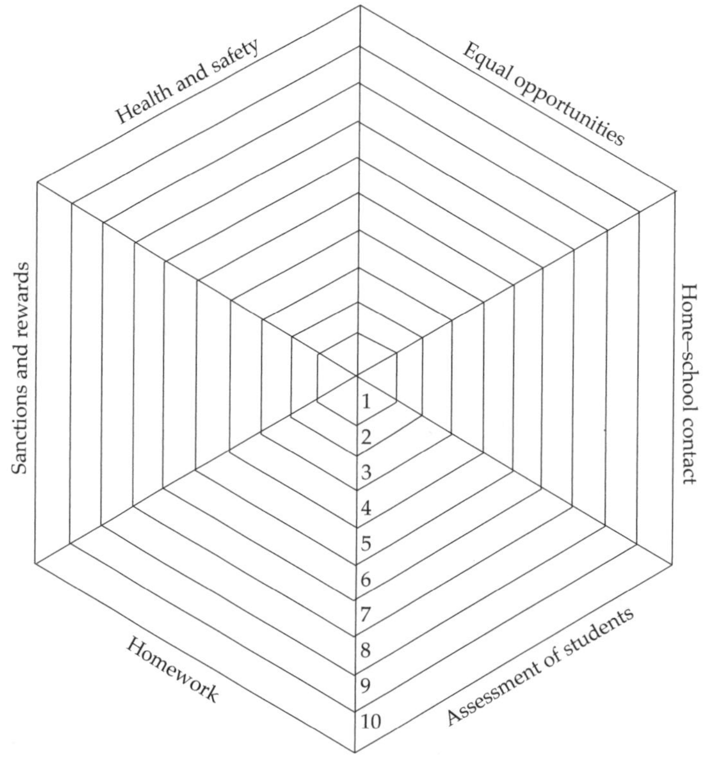

Figure A4.3 Defining school life

A regular analysis of costs is essential when ordering or changing priorities. The cost of bullying can be high, particularly when a complaint results in litigation. Most school staff would probably claim that their most valuable resource is time. Monitoring the expenditure of time may reveal – as many teachers have found – that a disproportionate amount is spent dealing with disciplinary matters, or on a particular individual. Here, pie charts are used to show the proportion of teachers' time spent on different activities (Figure A4.4).

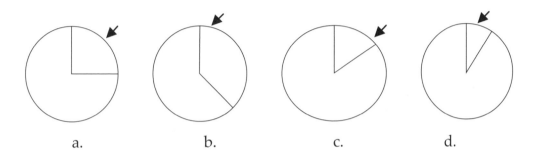

   a.   b.   c.   d.

   a. proportion of teacher's time during lessons spent on discipline.
   b. proportion of teacher's time outside lessons spent on discipline
   c. proportion of teacher's time spent on an individual student
   d. proportion of all reported incidents identified as bullying

Figure A4.4 Division of time in the working day

Appendix 5
A parents' checklist

Parents are clearly not in a position to assess their children's school as might their teachers. Although published information will guide their judgement, it is probably the basic human conditions that will give them the confidence to entrust their children to the school. The following checklist was compiled with parents and made available to all applicants to the school.

Reception

– Do the staff deal politely and efficiently with telephone enquiries?
– How are visitors received on arrival?
– Are visitors taken to where they need to go?

The general appearance of the premises

– Are they well maintained?
– Are they clean, tidy and free from litter?
– Is there graffiti?
– Are there pictures, plants, displays of students' work?
– Does the school look cared for?

The atmosphere

– Is it welcoming and friendly?
– Is it calm?
– Do students move in an orderly manner?
– Is there a general sense of purpose?

The facilities

– Are physical working conditions pleasant for students and staff?
– If congestion cannot be avoided, is it well controlled?
– Can students shelter from bad weather during breaks?
– Which parts of the premises are out of bounds?
– Is there a parents'/visitors' room?
– Is there quality catering?

Health and safety

– Is there a school nurse?
– Which hospital does the school use for emergencies or accidents?
– Is there proper protective equipment for such lessons as science and technology?
– Is there a safe road-crossing to the school?
– Are intruders a problem?

Parents and teachers probably share the view that the first rule for keeping young people out of trouble is to keep them occupied. There is a marked difference between those schools that cling to a familiar annual routine and those that look for fresh ideas, encourage new activities and offer new and varied educational opportunities. Students and their parents should expect the educational experience to be rich and rewarding. Here are some additional, general questions parents might ask.

– Are students shown examples of good work and behaviour?
– Are they kept busy?
– Do they show a keenness to learn?
– Are they encouraged to develop their own talents?
– Are they given a wide variety of learning situations?
– Are they challenged to do better?
– Do they have to make choices?
– Do they have the opportunity to develop personal relationships with other students and adults?
– Are they growing in confidence?
– Are they taught how to cope with change?
– Are they given a sense of values?
– Are they safe and healthy?
– Are they given responsibility?
– Do you feel that they are part of a caring community?
– Are they supported and guided when in difficulty?

Appendix 6
Letter to the press

An inner-city secondary school under special measures, with a declining role, local opposition and particular accusations of bullying, was further pilloried by both local and national press. The situation became critical when the school was named as one of the worst 18 in Britain. Fortunately, this concerted attack provoked an equally forceful reaction in defence of the school from students, LEA, Borough Council and others. The local press, changing its position, then began to contribute to the support being expressed:

> The Labour government has condemned the school as failing: but its views are based on outdated information. It has formed an opinion based on the last report carried out on the school: only 25 working days after the new team went in. That is totally unfair and can only damage the morale of everyone involved.

The following is an extract from a letter from the Head teacher to the local press, published under the headline 'Pity our neglected children'. The letter was written in defence of the school and its students, inspired by a student's protestation to a TV interviewer: 'We're tired of being told we're rubbish.'

> It is a worthwhile lesson from time to time to time to look at ourselves as others see us. The French philosopher, Voltaire, observing England and its government in the early part of the eighteenth century, wrote: 'There are about 800 people who are entitled to speak in public and uphold the nation's interests; about five or six thousand more who claim the same honour; all the rest pass judgement on them and everyone can publish what he thinks about public affairs. And that's why the whole country needs education.'
>
> This is not the eighteenth century and although we are not suffering the aftermath of a civil war, we do have a divided society. That is a dilemma as prominent in education as anywhere. As a nation, do we invest in all our children or in the selected few? The media, the self-styled experts and the politicians all tell us that education is in a mess. In reality, society is in a mess; it is in a state of decay and the most vivid evidence of its decline is in our treatment of children. There is not much point in blaming society, since society is intangible; so we blame schools. The family, the church, youth services, the expectation of a job for life are the crumbling pillars on which

children can no longer lean. It is the school that has become the last provider of continuity, stability and a framework of control. Children are uncertain about the future and fearful of a deteriorating environment.

There is a limit, nevertheless, to what schools can do. Education programmes on sex and drugs have not prevented the dramatic increase in sexual activity and drug abuse among the young. Education, law enforcement and a welfare society have not prevented the decline in moral standards or the prevalence of anti-social behaviour. Clearly, stronger influences are at work. Children are vulnerable to the influences of television, materialism, competitiveness and their undisclosed fears. In the face of these combined forces, schools can only inform; they cannot enforce. Teachers, nevertheless, have allowed themselves to take on full responsibility for the education, social and personal development of children and, if problems arise, teachers are condemned for their efforts. Their task is an impossible one. How illogical to judge a school by standards that should be set at home: behaviour, work, respect and self-esteem. More and more, the responsibility for children is being abandoned by adults. Cumulatively, this amounts to an alarming degree of neglect. How are children coping? We know that, like the young of all species, they are resilient, manipulative and opportunist; they are survivors. But they are confused by the mixed messages they receive from adults. We tell them not to drop litter, yet we are destroying the global environment. We tell them to be nice to one another, yet much of the entertainment we provide for them is violent. We tell them to value themselves, yet we are destructively materialistic. We promote hard work and independence and we play the Lottery.

Education in Britain today is like Gulliver: a powerful giant constrained by innumerable petty bonds. Stifling reforms and their associated bureaucracy have diverted teachers from essential tasks. Accelerating change has endangered levels of control and the lack of adequate investment is exploited by 'parasitic industries' that feed on the instability of the system. Schools are doing their best to counteract the effects of social disruption on children. Whatever criticisms are levelled at them, teachers have responded to reform and have recognised the importance of the part they play. They are battling against the odds to instil an appetite for learning and create the best possible conditions for progress and success. For the sake of students and teachers we have to find ways of putting enjoyment back into learning. This is more a matter of attitude than money. We must motivate children but children themselves must want to learn. They must understand that learning is not only useful, it is natural and it can be fun.

Appendix 7
'A typical day'

When schools have had what they might describe later as 'a typical day', it probably included change, pressure, problem solving and the unexpected. The cumulative effect of such working conditions is wearing for both staff and students. The breakdown of routine practices, substitute personnel for teaching and supervision, the movement of students to unfamiliar accommodation, a re-ordering of priorities, new demands made from outside are 'typical' for most schools. It is such conditions that commonly create an environment in which learning is curtailed and the doors are opened to disruptive behaviour. The following list is an actual record of one school's 'typical' day.

- At the beginning of the day, a notoriously disruptive student reports directly to the Head teacher that her class's substitute teacher has not arrived and no one has taken the register.
- An ambulance is called to a student with suspected appendicitis.
- A police officer arrives to alert the school to an air-gun incident in the vicinity of the school.
- Flooding caused by a burst water pipe outside the school prevents entry through the main entrance.
- A parent insists on seeing the Head teacher to urge the replacement of an English teacher on long-term absence.
- A senior management briefing is re-scheduled to the end of the school day.
- Contact is made with the local newspaper with a view to offering a regular feature about the school's activities.
- Several telephone calls are received from the LEA and professional associations regarding the latest educational reform on funding.
- Teaching staff call for urgent negotiations in respect of cover for absent colleagues.
- The school is asked to nominate two teachers to attend a negotiating skills course.
- A case of hepatitis among the staff is reported.
- A parent/governor continues to make persistent demands on behalf of her daughter who, the parent claims, needs extra support.
- The school librarian reports her purse stolen.
- A student is mugged on her way home from school.

Bibliography

Arora, C. M. J. and Thompson, D. A. (1987) *My Life in School Checklist.* Windsor, UK: NFER-Nelson.

Bayliss, V. (1999) *Opening Minds – Education for the 21st century.* London: Royal Society of Arts.

British Broadcasting Corporation, Broadcasting Standards Commission and Independent Television Commission (1998) *Report of the Joint Working Party on Violence on Television.* London: BBC, BSC and ITC Joint Working Party.

Brown, S. (2001) *The Invisible Dimension: A teacher's handbook for violence prevention.* Liverpool: Liverpool Education and Lifelong Learning Service.

Calouste Gulbenkian Foundation Commission on Children and Violence (1995) *Children and Violence.* London: Calouste Gulbenkian Foundation.

Calouste Gulbenkian Foundation (2000) *Passport – A framework for personal and social development.* London: Calouste Gulbenkian Foundation.

Calouste Gulbenkian Foundation (2001) *UK Review of Effective Government Structures for Children 2001* (edited by Hodgkin, R. and Newell, P.). London: Calouste Gulbenkian Foundation.

Charity Commission (2002) *Regulatory Study RS1 – Trustees, Recruitment, Selection and Induction.* London: Charity Commission.

Children are Unbeatable Alliance (2000) *Response to the Department of Health's Consultation Document on the Physical Punishment of Children.* London: National Association for the Prevention of Cruelty to Children.

Cowie, H., Jennifer, D. and Sharp, S. (2001) 'Tackling violence in schools', a report from the 'CONNECT' – UK. *Tackling Violence in Schools on a European Basis CONNECT Country Report.* Surrey, UK: Roehampton University of Surrey.

DES (1989) *Discipline in Schools* (The Elton Report). London: HMSO.

DfEE (1999a) *National Healthy School Standard – Getting started.* London: DfEE.

DfEE (1999b) *All Our Futures.* London: DfEE.

DfES (2001) *National Pupil Absence Table.* London: DfES.

Docking, J. and MacGrath, M. (2002) *Managing Behaviour in the Primary School,* 3rd edn. London: Falmer.

ESRC (Economic and Social Research Council) (2002) *A View from the Girls: Exploring violence and violent behaviour.* Violence Research Programme. London: ESRC.

Griffith, R. (2000) *National Curriculum: National disaster.* London: Routledge/Falmer.

Hansard (2002) 24 April, Columns 309, 310, 315, 332. London: The Stationery Office.

Hewitt, R. L. (2001) *The Violence-resilient School: A comparative study of schools and their environments.* London: Economic and Social Research Council.

Kids' Clubs Network (2000) *Centres for Curiosity and Imagination – A guide to creating wonder.* London: Kids' Clubs Network (Trading) Ltd.

Kitching, R. and Morgan, S. (2001) *Violence, Truancy and School Exclusion in France and Britain.* London: Franco-British Council.

Lamplugh, D. and Pagan, B. (2000) *Safewise – Developing safer independence.* London: The Suzy Lamplugh Trust and the National Confederation of Parent Teacher Associations.

Mental Health Foundation (1999) *The Big Picture.* London: Mental Health Foundation.

National Association of Head Teachers (2000) *Guidance on Bullying.* Haywards Heath, UK: Hobsons PLC on behalf of NAHT.

NSPCC (National Society for the Prevention of Cruelty to Children) (2002) *First Check – A toolkit for organisations to safeguard children.* London: NSPCC.

NUT (National Union of Teachers) (1998) *Tackling Harassment and Bullying in Schools.* London: NUT.

Newell, P. (2000) *Taking Children Seriously.* London: Calouste Gulbenkian Foundation.

OfSTED (2001) *Improving Attendance and Behaviour in Secondary Schools, A report from Her Majesty's Chief Inspector of Schools.* London: HMSO.

Olweus, D. (1993) *Bullying at School.* Bergen, Norway: University of Bergen.

QCA (Qualifications and Curriculum Authority) (2000a) *Personal, Social and Health Education and Citizenship at Key Stages 1 and 2: Initial guidance for schools.* Sudbury, UK: QCA Publications.

QCA (Qualifications and Curriculum Authority) (2000b) *Citizenship at Key Stages 3 and 4.* Sudbury, UK: QCA Publications.

QCA (Qualifications and Curriculum Authority) (2000c) *Personal, Social and Health Education at Key Stages 3 and 4.* Sudbury, UK: QCA Publications.

Sport England (2002) *Safeguarding Children in Sport.* Leicester: National Society for the Prevention of Cruelty to Children (NSPCC).

Summerskill, B. (2002) 'Bullying rife in Britain's "caring" jobs', *Observer*, 12 May, p. 4.

United Nations (1990) *Convention on the Rights of the Child.* New York: United Nations.

Varnava, G. (2000) *Towards a Non-violent Society – Checkpoints for schools.* London: National Children's Bureau/Forum on Children and Violence.

Varnava, G. (2002) *Towards a Non-violent Society – Checkpoints for young people.* London: National Children's Bureau/Forum on Children and Violence.

Wolf, J. (1999) 'Nation of shopkeepers that knows how to flog', *Times Educational Supplement*, 31 December.

Zero Tolerance Trust (1999) *Report on the Attitude Towards Violence and Women.* Edinburgh: Zero Tolerance Trust.

Index